PLANTS & GARDENS

BROOKLYN BOTANIC GARDEN RECORD

Gardening for Fragrance

1989

Brooklyn Botanic Garden

Staff for this issue:

TANIA BAYARD, *Guest Editor*

BARBARA B. PESCH, *Editor*

CHARLES GABELER, *Art Director*

JO KEIM, *Associate Editor*

and the Editorial Committee of the Brooklyn Botanic Garden

DONALD E. MOORE, *President, Brooklyn Botanic Garden*

ELIZABETH SCHOLTZ, *Director Emeritus*

STEPHEN K-M. TIM, *Vice President, Science & Publications*

First printing, September 1989
Second printing, February 1992

PLANTS & GARDENS

BROOKLYN BOTANIC GARDEN RECORD

Gardening for Fragrance

Vol. 45   Handbook #121   Fall 1989   No. 3

CONTENTS

All Photographs by Elvin McDonald unless otherwise indicated

Plants and Gardens, Brooklyn Botanic Garden Record (ISSN 0362-5850) is published quarterly at 1000 Washington Ave., Brooklyn, N.Y. 11225, by the **Brooklyn Botanic Garden, Inc.** Second-class-postage paid at Brooklyn, N.Y., and at additional mailing offices. Subscriptions included in Botanic Garden membership dues ($25.00 per year), which includes newsletters and announcements. Copyright © 1989, 1992 by the Brooklyn Botanic Garden, Inc.
POSTMASTER: Send address changes to BROOKLYN BOTANIC GARDEN, Brooklyn, N.Y. 11225
ISBN #0-945352-54-9

foreword

According to legend, when God banished Adam from Paradise He allowed him to take away three plants: wheat, the principal food; the date, the most delicious fruit; and myrtle, the queen of scented flowers. From earliest times plants have been esteemed as much for their fragrance as for their practical value.

Today, Adam could sniff a perfumed advertisement in a glossy magazine or breathe air scented by an electric scent dispenser, but, he might prefer to cultivate his own fragrances. And the scented plants in his garden would no doubt make him homesick for the Garden of Eden, for smell is the sense most closely tied to memory. Perhaps one of the reasons why fragrant plants are loved and cultivated by gardeners everywhere is that they so insistently bring back the joys of childhood. Some of my most cherished memories of my father's garden are the delicate smell of rainbow-colored sweet peas, the tangy odor of tomato plants warmed by the sun, and the pungent aroma of zinnias, marigolds and nasturtiums filling the house when all the late-blooming flowers had been gathered before the first frost.

Throughout history plant scents have delighted and served humankind. The ancient Greeks and Romans wove sweet-smelling herbs such as rosemary, oregano, mint, bay, and thyme into garlands, and they also strewed these herbs on their floors so that the lovely fragrances would dispel bad odors and cheer the heart. For deodorants the Greeks rubbed mint on their arms and wore necklaces made of pomanders of rose petals, Indian nard, and myrrh. In the Middle Ages mint and rosemary were used to sweeten the breath; lavender, rose petals, and the roots of valerian were laid away with clothes to perfume them; and in the heat of the summer, bunches of sweet woodruff were hung in houses to freshen the air. Strong-smelling herbs like wormwood, southernwood, tansy and rosemary have long served as moth repellants; and rue, with its acrid smell, was once strewn about as a disinfectant, particularly in English law courts, where it was thought to protect the judges from jail fever. The Welsh in the 6th century are said to have worn leeks in their caps so that their stench would repel the invading Anglo-Saxons. The odors of some plants have been considered harmful: the heavy, sweet scent of the narcissus, for example, was once reputed to cause lethargy and madness. The scent of violets, however, was thought to be salubrious; according to a medieval health manual one only had to smell these lovely flowers to feel well.

Today we understand a great deal more about the botanical and chemical aspects of fragrance than did our ancestors. But modern scientific developments have not been entirely positive. While chemists can concoct all kinds of artificial scents in test tubes, hybridizers have succeeded in breeding the fragrances out of many flowers that were once treasured as much for their smell as for their appearance. There is renewed interest in natural fragrances, however, as is evidenced by the numerous fragrance gardens that have sprung up around the country and the many books now on the market devoted to scented plants. It is hoped that the articles in this handbook will stimulate further enthusiasm and encourage gardeners everywhere to discover the pleasures of gardening for fragrance.

Tania Bayard is a free-lance writer, lecturer, horticulturist and art historian. She has written several books and is in the process of writing two more. This is the first time she has guest edited for BBG. She divides her time between Manhattan and Vermont.

Roses and rose petals collected to make potpourri create a tapestry of colors and textures and a rich blend of fragrances.

Tania Bayard
Guest Editor

Biological Aspects of Scent

Doris Stone

Flowering plants are the most versatile chemical factories on earth. Not only do they synthesize food for themselves and the entire animal kingdom, but they also produce a whole range of other compounds, formerly thought to be mere waste products of this intense chemical activity. Only in the last few decades has it become apparent that these so-called waste products have genuine survival value. Thus odors attract pollinators or repel predators, while unpleasant-tasting substances, often downright poisons, prevent plants from being grazed to death. In other words, during the course of evolution the development of co–relationships between plants and animals — including interdependence — became the key to biological success. Here we are concerned only with plant odors, but other substances such as nectar, pollen, pigments and poisonous alkaloids were part of the story.

The process of coevolution began some 100 to 150 million years ago. The scents of flowering plants became geared to the animals evolving at the same time, namely the mammals and the insects. The formula for success: plant odors that activate animal olfactory organs and animal behavior programmed to respond to these odors, either positively or negatively.

Flowering plant odors are mainly associated with sexual reproduction, and the necessary prelude to seed production is pollination of the flower. Enlisting animal help with pollination demanded plant lures. Food is the ultimate lure, but its presence had to be advertised. Scent, color, and flower form proved to be the most efficacious method. Modifications of plant and animal morphology evolved "in tandem," ensuring a unique kind of mutualism, whereby pollination is assured by payment of rewards.

The production of odors is expensive to the plant — indicating that it is needed to ensure survival. For instance, within the inflorescences of the arums, both temperate and tropical, starch is consumed and the respiration rate increases with the subsequent generation of heat. Volatile substances (evil-smelling to our noses) are emitted, attracting to the plant hordes of pollinating flies. Familiar examples of such flowers are the two skunk cabbage species of the eastern and western states.

What is the nature of these floral scents? All are volatile organic compounds and most are "essential oils" in that their essences can be extracted by steam distillation or with ether. Chemically, they are terpenes — thus geraniol from the rose is a monoterpene and β-ionone from the violet is a sesquiterpene. There are also aromatic volatiles, such as vanillin from many orchids. Some are amines and other unpleasant-smelling compounds — at least to us and to bees — but more of this later. Many hundreds of these substances are known and indeed any particular flower scent may consist of around a hundred of these constituents. No wonder floral scents are individual and distinctive to a particular species. Think of the complex smell of gardenia or of lavender.

The fragrance is produced by special parts of the petals, which bear secretory glands (see diagram of the cross-section of a petal as seen under the microscope). In fact, it has been recently shown that not only honey guides (more correctly called nectar guides) but scent guides also direct insects to the food source within the flower. Usually, the location

Doris Stone, botanist and horticulturist, former Director of Education at the Brooklyn Botanic Garden, is the author of Great Public Gardens of the Eastern United States *(Pantheon, 1982) and* The Lives of Plants *(Scribner's, 1983).*

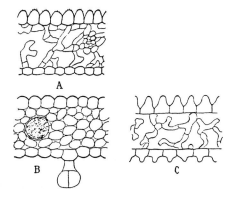

Cross sections of petals: A, Amelanchier laevis; B, Lysimachia nummularia, *showing glandular hair and secretory chamber;* C, Pinguicula vulgaris.

of both types of guide coincide, reinforcing one another. In young horsechestnut blossoms, for instance, the nectar guides are yellow and scented, but with age they turn crimson, lose their scent, and stop nectar production. (Bee color vision is not as sensitive to crimson as to yellow.) Because of these changes bees do not waste energy on flowers already pollinated.

Timing of scent-production is economical as well as an adaptation to the clientèle. Blooms catering to night-flying animals, such as moths and bats, smell only at night, while flowers pollinated by diurnal insects give off their strongest perfume at noon. In general, scent production ceases after pollination.

Among flowers that attract night-fliers are honeysuckle, gardenia, stock, tobacco, tuberose and evening primrose. One tropical plant of the tobacco family, *Cestrum nocturnum,* produces such a strong "heady" odor that it cannot be grown near the house. Its Sudanese name means 'night whore' ("unobtrusive in the daytime, agreeable at night, and disgusting in the morning!").[1]

It appears that in the early years of floral evolution scent rather than color was the primary attractant. Pollinators were beetles — then at the peak of insect evolution — and though they have good "noses," their color vision is poor. Today's primitive flowers — magnolias, water lilies, peonies and members of the custard apple family Annonaceae — are strongly scented and still beetle-pollinated.[2] Some offer only pollen — beetles cannot cope

with nectar. Subsequently, as bees, butterflies and moths began to appear, so did new floral forms in the "tandem" evolution already mentioned.

It is indeed fortunate for us that odors attractive to most pollinators are also attractive to us, or else the world would be a less pleasant place to live in. But for the insect, floral scents elicit a foraging response, their sources to be tracked down. The olfactory sense of honeybees has been studied more intensively than that of other insects. In its acuity and its preferences it is much like our own. Thus the thresholds for detecting scent are about the same in the two species, around 1.9×10^9 to 4.5×10^{11} molecules per cm^3. Contrast this with the incredible sensitivity of the dog's nose — 6,000 mols. per cm^3 of butyric acid (hence the success of bloodhounds, this acid being found in human sweat).

Bees can readily be trained to fly to a food source, if it is "labeled" with a particular scent, which has to be pleasant and flowery. They cannot be trained to an unpleasant smell, such as that of rotting meat. The food source is usually sugar water, which lacks any smell of its own. After the training period these guinea pig bees are now let loose in an area where there are twenty-four pleasant and flowery scents. Invariably they fly to the scent they have been trained to, indicating a high degree of olfactory discrimination. If the bees are trained to a mixture of two flowery scents and later tested with the separate components, they will fly to both. But the most extraordinary finding was that bees can be trained to a particular *sequence* of three scents. In a tube baited with sugar water the scent at the mouth was rosemary, followed by thyme and lastly, fennel. After a training period the bees were presented with four similar tubes. Only one was identical to the original tube. The other three held the *same* scents but in different sequences. Of the hundred or so bees in the experiment, approximately 80 chose the tube

[1] *Reference — Barth — see Bibliography*
[2] *When I was plant breeder of magnolias at BBG these beetles, no more than 5mm long, were my competitors!*

7

with the "correct" sequence. An astonishing result — involving not only olfactory discrimination, but memory of space/time experiences as well.

Within the hive the scents of flowers currently in bloom are given off by the bodies of the returning collectors. This information, together with the location of the flowers (conveyed by the famous "waggle dance" of these same collectors[*3]), allows the neophyte worker bees to embark on their "maiden" trips unescorted. Once outside the hive, guided by the sun, they fly towards the target. From a distance flower color attracts, but then, as they turn into the wind, it is the scent that finally brings them to the food source. Nectar and scent guides lead them and/or their probosces past the stamens and pistil to the nectar awaiting them in the floral depths.

For decades, if not centuries, naturalists have been impressed with the so-called flower constancy of bees — the fact that within a particular area bees stick with the same species of flower until all individuals have been visited. Obviously, with limited time and energy it is much more efficient to repeat the same maneuvers on the same type of flower over and over again. Once the idiosyncrasies of a type of flower, say a foxglove or an oregano, have been learned, foraging is greatly speeded up. And, from the plants' point of view, flower constancy is essential. Seed set can only come about if pollen of the same species is deposited on the female organ or pistil. Were bees to dart about from one type of flower to another they would be failures as pollinators.

Only recently has it been proved that the bee identifies the particular species, not by its shape nor its color, but by its distinctive scent. After all, if a hundred or so ingredients can go into the manufacture of a particular floral perfume, and given the bee's olfactory acuity, mistakes are unlikely. In fact, of the various signals bees associate with flowers, scent is learned more rapidly than either color or form and is

[3*] *First discovered by Karl von Frisch — see B. J. D. Meeuse* Pollination, *Carolina Biology Reader #33.*

Photos by Doris Stone

Cabbage white butterfly hovering over a cabbage. The leaves have holes in them indicating the presence of caterpillars as well.

probably an innate fixture in the nervous system. To sum up, flower constancy is a nice example of mutualism on the ecological scene.

Zoologists, involved in the study of pollination ecology, have in recent years studied the bee's olfactory organ. As most of us would guess, its "nose" comprises the two antennae that stick out from its head. Microscopic (both light and electron) examinations have revealed that each antenna is dotted with about 6,000 oval, concave pore plates or sensilla, which are connected with special sense cells. Approximately 3,500 tiny pores on each pore plate allow air to diffuse through, and, if scent-laden, the air excites first the sense cells and then the brain. The two antennae can detect odors separately — an advantage the bee has over us. This is no doubt related to the important role of smell in its locomotion. The antennae of flies, beetles, butterflies and moths play a similar role in detecting smells. Flies, however, tend to be attracted to what we would term unpleasant odors, which brings us to the topic of the stinking flowers.

Mentioned earlier was the family Araceae, whose tubular inflorescences give off volatile amines, smelling of stinking fish, feces or rotting flesh. In the plant world this is deceptive advertising. Expecting a rotting organic medium for egg-laying, flies become entrapped in the floral tube, and willy-nilly effect pollination as they gorge pollen or nectar (or lay eggs) during their temporary incarceration. Death of floral tissues allows their escape; undaunted and pollen-dusted they fly off to the next arum to be similarly fooled.

The putrid smell of Jack-in-the-pulpit or skunk cabbage is nothing compared to that of some exotic arums. Thus the Sardinian arum *Helicodiceros muscivorus,* only 15 inches high, releases a stench in quantity and quality equal to that emitted by the corpse of a sheep. The Indonesian *Amorphophallus titanum* with an inflorescence eight feet high, can emit such an overpowering stink that squeamish bystanders have been known to faint!

Color also plays a part in luring flies and beetles to these evil-smelling flowers — their spathes or petals are often the maroon color of decaying meat. Still, the arums do reward the insects with some kind of sustenance; but not so the members of the *Stapelia* genus of African succulents. Lured to the starfish-shaped flowers by color and the odor of bad fish, the flies go unrewarded. Larvae that hatch from the eggs foolishly laid on the maroon petals will face starvation. Nothing mutualistic about this — the flies are duped to serve the plants' ends.

Another form of plant exploitation is even more bizarre. It occurs in the genus *Ophrys,* comprising small orchids mainly confined to the Mediterranean region, but also occurring worldwide. Each *Ophrys* flower looks like a female insect sitting on a flower — a fly, a spider or many species of bee orchids — the name indicating the type of insect simulated. This is the visual lure, but the olfactory one is even more powerful, as was proved by a botanist who hid one flower in his parked car with open windows! It is the sexual pheromone (or a very good chemical mimic of it) of the female and it is *manufactured by the orchid.* In spring the males hatch before the females, so these deceiving flowers have no competition from the "real thing." Pollination is accomplished by a pseudocopulation on the flower. Then unsatisfied (as one might guess) the pollen-bearing male goes off to "mate" with another *Ophrys.* No nectar is offered and the pollen is inaccessible as food as it is contained in structures called pollinia, which stick to the insect's body during the encounter.

I once found a wild bee orchid on the English Downs. Its color, markings, hairiness and shape were quite remarkable. Yet this orchid is self pollinated; it is beyond the range of the solitary bee or wasp that originally pollinated it (its seeds having been transported by some means from the Mediterranean). This, of course, is the danger of depending on just one type of pollinator. Extinction was avoided in this case, but not all flowers are capable of self pollination.

Another strange relationship between orchids and male euglossine bees occurs in the tropical forests of central and South America. This is one of mutualism in that the bees collect perfume made by the flower and in so doing pollinate them. Called "magnificent bees" in German because of their resplendent blue/green/gold colors, they are related to bumble bees, except that they have exceptionally long tongues. During their solitary existence they feed on the nectar of butterfly

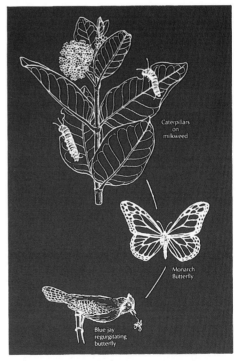

Caterpillars on milkweed

Monarch Butterfly

Blue jay regurgitating butterfly

The above illustrations show the exploitation of milkweed (Asclepias *sp*) *by the monarch butterfly.*

9

flowers, but just before courtship they are attracted to certain orchids by their powerful perfumes (each species of bee seems to have its own orchid preference).

The scent is collected from the flower and stored in special spongy "perfume flasks," located on the tibiae of the hind legs. One species of bee can store 60 mm³ of the odor substance, the main ingredient of which is a eucalyptus essential oil. No food is available. Often the scent is intoxicating, pollination being achieved as the bees flounder about within the flower.

Male bees with full perfume flasks now congregate in swarms or "leks," ventilate themselves with fluttering wings, as if attempting to waft the scent around. For some reason the females are attracted to the swarms and mating occurs. It cannot be just the perfume because female bees do not visit the orchids, which are exclusive male "clubs." The peculiar sex habits of these orchid bees was elucidated only some fifteen years ago by C. H. Dodgson and S. Vogel.

Alluring odors are mainly the province of flowers but there is at least one carnivorous plant that, by means of the mousy smell of the alkaloid coniine, attracts flies. It is *Sarracenia flava,* the American pitcher plant. Not only does the smell lure the insects into the trap, but the poison paralyses them, making capture and digestion that much easier. (Also present in the leaves of hemlock *Conium maculatum,* it was the poison given to Socrates.)

Currently, with the popularity of low-salt diets, back-to-nature recipes and remedies, herbs, and especially culinary ones, are highly fashionable. What exactly is the biological purpose of all these aromatic substances, mainly essential oils, that abound in the leaf glands of mint, dill, sage, bay laurel, tarragon, chives, garlic, thyme, lovage, catnip, artemisia, scented geraniums, etc.? Little scientific research has been carried out, but from what puny evidence we have they appear to be deterrents to leaf-eating predators, especially insects. If you have a herb garden, you may have noticed how relatively free it is of insect diseases, compared with your vegetable garden.

We do know that mint deters mice (reference[4] below). And in 1964 T. Eisner, in nicely controlled experiments, showed that though felines regard catnip as a felicitous gift from the gods, ants find it just the reverse. Having extracted the essential oil of catnip, nepetalactone, he isolated a group of ants, using a glass rod dipped in the liquid to circumscribe a circle. The ants refused to cross this nepetalactone "moat." Moreover, if a drop of the oil is placed in the path of ants advancing upon their food, they make a wide detour to avoid it. Dr. Eisner took two corpses of cockroaches, which they readily eat, impregnated one with nepetalactone and left both close to an ant colony. Soon the uncontaminated roach was swarming with ants, while the other was left virtually alone. Besides ants, other insects are repelled by the catnip oil, among them beetles and spittlebugs.

These insects do not, however, function as pollinators of herb flowers. An alternative view of these essential oils exists — though perhaps the two theories are not mutually exlusive. This theory holds that the scented leaves enhance the attractiveness of the usually inconspicuous flowers. I have noticed that when oregano is in bloom no other flower in my garden is so popular with honeybees, despite the flowers' small size and pink color, which is certainly not one of the so-called bee colors. Are the oregano flowers specially rich in nectar? If so,and assuming that the worker bees have learned this fact within the hive, then the essential oils of the entire plant may serve collectively as a compelling floral attractant. Testimony to the success of the pollination process is the number of oregano seedings that spring up all over my herb garden every spring.

With few exceptions fragrance is associated with all kinds of fruits. Ripe fleshy ones are especially fragrant when bruised by falling to the ground or by being jostled by foraging

[4] Leaves — *Ghillean Tolmie Prance & Kjell B. Sandved.*

animals. Are these odors a means of attracting animals to succulent tidbits, so that the seeds get dispersed? It would seem so. Surely the essential oils present in the peel of citrus (oil of bergamot is used to scent commodities as diverse as soap, tea and perfume), the delectable smell of ripe strawberries, apricots, and plums, are not merely fortuitous? The seeds of the larger fruits are usually rejected, but those of the smaller ones are known to pass through the digestive tract unharmed. In the case of the small aromatic dry fruits of umbellifers (Apiaceae) such as anise, coriander, dill and parsley, presumably the number of seeds destroyed by chewing is offset by those lost in transit (like the acorn).

Thus throughout the whole sexual reproductive process of the flowering plants, scents play an important role in recruiting animal help.

On the other hand plant odors do not always function as attractants — many serve to stop predators in their tracks. Instead of poisoning the animal outright, they provide olfactory warnings that the herbivores immediately heed. Should an insect, for example, begin to chew the leaves of a wild cherry *(Prunus serotina, P. caroliniana),* it will immediately detect the smell of bitter almonds — hydrocyanic acid, a lethal nerve poison. A glucose compound stored in the leaf cells breaks up on exposure to oxygen of the air, liberating the fatal gas. In the cabbage family all the leaves contain sinigrin. Again damage to the cells, allowing the entry of air, causes the substance to decompose, liberating the insecticide mustard oil. (It is interesting to note that although hydrocyanic acid is fatal to man, mustard oil is a revered condiment — in small quantities. But we have to remember that in the early days of flowering plant evolution, insects, as predators, were the greatest enemies — not our own species.) Since insects are the most adaptable of animals there are always some species of insects that develop immunity to plant poisons. Witness the cabbage white caterpillars and cabbage aphids that voraciously thrive on all brassicas and will even die without their favor-

ite sinigrin! These are just two of the many aromatic poisons liberated by plants when attacked by hungry herbivores. Some of the old medieval names for weeds such as henbane, dogbane, cowbane, fleabane and wolfsbane indicate that such feeding deterrents are widespread — none of the above plants belong to the same family ('bane' is of course an old English word for poison).

There is no doubt that the flowering plant is a parfumerie par excellence, and though we have elucidated the roles of some of the odors emitted there are still many basic questions needing answers. Coordination of the biochemistry involved is a closed book. What, for instance, triggers the wonderful fragrance of honeysuckle at dusk on a summer's evening? The question is simple, but the complicated answer has yet to come from the relatively new science of ecological biochemistry. ❧

Bibliography

Barth, Frederich G. *Insects and Flowers: The Biology of a Partnership.* Princeton, N.J.: Princeton Univ. Press. 1985.

Faegri, K. & van der Pijl. *Principles of Pollination Ecology.* 3rd. Ed. Elmsford, N.Y.: Pergamon Press. 1979.

Harborne, J.B. *Introduction to Biological Biochemistry.* 2nd. Ed. New York: Harcourt Brace Jovanovich. Academic Press. 1982.

Holm, Eigil. *Biology of Flowers.* A Penguin Nature Guide. Harmondsworth, Middlesex. England: Penguin Books. 1979.

Prance, Ghillean Tolmie, and Kjell B. Sandved. *Leaves.* New York: Crown Publishers, Inc. 1984.

Meeuse, B. and Morris, Sean. *The Sex Life of Flowers.* New York: Facts on File Publications. 1984.

Meeuse, B.J.D. *Pollination.* Burlington, North Carolina: Carolina Biology Reader no. 33. 1984.

Meeuse, B.J.D. *The Story of Pollination.* New York: The Ronald Press Co. 1961.

Stone, Doris M. *The Lives of Plants.* New York: Charles Scribner's Sons. 1983.

THE LORE AND LURE OF PERFUME

Frank Anderson

Perfume has always been one of the grace notes of civilization. Beginning in ancient Egypt, where it was employed to enhance royal and religious ceremonies, the use of perfume soon spread into other areas of everyday life. Long before such concepts as botany and chemistry came into being, aromatic substances were widely popular, and trade routes that brought them to market had been well established. Rather than the flagons of fragrant liquids to which we are accustomed, perfumes were originally distributed in the form of incense, scented oils, resins, gums, and fragrant wood. As for flowers, although everyone took pleasure in smelling them, such enjoyment was short lived, generally confined to the place and the season that actually produced the blossoms, for no means of preserving their elusive odors existed as yet.

All of that changed, however, with the chance observation that heavily scented flowers transferred their aroma to fatty substances, such as tallow or greasy hides. In all probability some highly fragrant blossoms came into lengthy, accidental contact with solidified fats in a sequestered storage area. The result was the discovery of *enfleurage,* the technique of placing petals upon layers of

Frank Anderson is the author of numerous botanical books, including An Illustrated History of the Herbals *(Columbia University Press, 1977) and the two-volume* Herbals Through 1500 *(Abaris Books, 1983 and 1984). He is Honorary Curator of Rare Books and Manuscripts at the New York Botanical Garden.*

fat until their volatile oils are completely absorbed, a practice that remains in use to this day in the perfume industry.

Various combinations were tried out, once the principle was recognized, and previous experience gained in the preparation of incense, or the preservation of mummies, was fully exploited. Luckily Egypt had a rich selection of aromatic essences, and before long a torrent of unguents and pomades filled the cosmetic jars of the land. Men and women alike fell victims to the craze, and it became unthinkable to hold any private feast or ceremony without offering cones of fragrant pomade to all the household guests. The manner of use, however, was hardly to the modern taste, as the cones were perched atop the heads of the assembly, where they slowly melted and trickled down into their wigs or hair. Not only did this require the balancing skills of a juggler, but there was also apt to be a messy conclusion, once the abundance of wine and beer began to have its effect on the revellers.

Thebes, 19th Dynasty, c 1275 B.C. Ipuy and his wife receiving offerings from their children— note fragrance cones. Egyptian Expedition of The Metropolitan Museum of Art, Rogers Fund, 1930. (30.4.114)

Despite the wealth of fragrance at the Egyptians' disposal, recurring shortages of certain items interfered with some rituals. Worship of the god Amon demanded inordinate amounts of frankincense to be burned in his temples, more in fact than was obtainable by ordinary means. In 1560 B.C. Queen Hatshepsut set about rectifying that situation, and sent a small expedition to the land of Punt at the mouth of the Red Sea. There 31 *Boswellia carteri* trees were purchased and safely transported back to Egypt, thus ending the incense crisis. That also initiated the first record of botanical exploration and plant introduction, since it was depicted among the sculptures on the walls of Hatshepsut's temple at Deir el-Bahri, just west of Thebes.

The development of the craft of perfumery was by no means confined to ancient Egypt. The Babylonians, Assyrians, Greeks, Romans, and then the Arabs all made continuous contributions. Besides *enfleurage,* there were the techniques of expression, wherein essential oils were forced out by the application of pressure, just as is done in an olive mill, and also maceration. In the latter process pieces of plants are broken up and placed in heated oil or fat. Roses, violets, cassie flowers from species of acacia, and orange blossoms are usually treated in this way. Yet another method is to use solvents to extract the essential oils of the flowers — generally petroleum ether, which is later distilled off. A partially solid substance, called the *concrete,* remains, and that, in turn, is subjected to alcohol, followed by freezing or filtering to remove all of the remaining plant waxes. Finally the alcohol is eliminated, and a highly concentrated perfumed oil, the *absolute,* becomes the chief tool of the perfumer in the creation of newly blended aromas. At long last the evasiveness of scent has been brought under control, but the process does exact a price, which is why perfumes become an increasingly expensive luxury.

To combat rising costs, natural aromatics are being replaced by synthetic ones, yet there is a limit to the deceits that can be practiced on the nose. Some degree of natural material is required if the scent is to remain free of the sharper notes that are born in the chemist's flask rather than in a flower's corolla. To provide such natural aromas there must be a place where flowers can be raised and harvested, perhaps even partially processed. But it is precisely there that the perfumer's world encounters the destructive forces of economics. Raising flowers means having access to parcels of land, and in a world where food shortages are becoming acute, pleasant smells are low on the priority list. What is more, housing is as greedy for land as farming, and more and more marginal and remote areas are being placed under cultivation. Where huge tracts of land once supported the raising of flowers for seed or scent materials, the floral trades are today being brought to the edge of extinction. We must now go to such locations as Reunion Island, in the Indian Ocean, or the hinterlands of Morocco, to find enough soil to produce the necessary crops. As matters stand at present the flower growers are being driven from California, much as they were from Grasse, France, where perfume materials are still processed but no longer produced.

Over the course of centuries certain animal substances were found to be highly preservative of scent—musk, civet, and ambergris being well known examples. The musk deer of Asia was even brought to the edge of extinction by avaricious hunters who killed this rare animal simply for the sake of its scent glands, discarding all the rest of the carcass. Much the same was true of the civet cat, and the only reason that whales were not destroyed for their ambergris was because they generally voided the material at sea, and there was no certainty that they retained any useful amounts concealed within their digestive tracts. In any event, modern chemistry has provided satisfactory substitutes, fixatives that bind the volatile oils, releasing their aromatic properties very slowly over long periods of time. The procedure is roughly akin to the way in which pine needles encapsulate and gradually exude their content of fragrant resin.

One plant product which has been used increasingly of late is oak moss, *mousse de chêne,* which is in fact a lichen. When first gathered it is seemingly odorless, but placed in storage it soon begins to develop a heavy, penetrating aroma that has the invaluable ability to blend well with other odors. The scent arises from the lichen's production of oleoresins, which not only possess a pleasing smell, but also greatly retard loss of essential oils through volatility, actually filling the function of a fixative.

Among aromatic oddities is the "odor of sanctity," which is genuine enough, although not properly classifiable as a perfume ingredient. Long thought to be the result of having led a particularly devout life, it is now known to be caused by nothing more sacrosanct than bacterial action. Bacteria, after all, do comprise a separate division of the plant kingdom, essentially the same as the flowers that bloom in the fields. Very often they accompany certain courses of illness such as diabetes or tuberculosis and profoundly affect the scent of the breath, the skin and various bodily secretions. Should the bacillus *pyocyaneus* be present the aroma of strawberries will be noticed, and since strawberries were long associated with paradise as the fruits of good deeds, it is clear how the general assumption of the odor of holiness came about. In instances where turpentine has been used to cleanse the body the smell of violets becomes pronounced, while other scents, as lily, rose, and pineapple, have also been noted.

There has been a strong connection since ancient times between health and highly aromatic substances, a connection that modern science reinforces to a considerable degree. Many of the essential oils used in perfumery possess powerful bactericidal properties. It was not entirely for nothing that pomanders and nosegays were carried and frequently sniffed in public assemblages, almost down to present times. In addition to masking obnoxious odors with pungent and pleasant ones, the essences inhaled had an antiseptic effect on undesirable bacteria. The Institut Pasteur of Paris eventually examined the observation that workers in the flower growing areas of France seemed less susceptible to tuberculosis than inhabitants of other locations. Exposure to essential oils was rightly deemed to be the cause, and among the most effective were found to be cinnamon, cloves, verbena, lavender, juniper, cedar, thyme, lemon, pine and wormwood. The practices of the Middle Ages were vindicated to a considerable degree by this discovery, and the effectiveness of thieves' vinegar was partially confirmed. The latter was a concoction of rosemary, sage, and pungent herbs steeped in sharp vinegar, and it was believed to repel plague. It was sprinkled about by those intending to plunder houses vacated by the plague stricken, but it was *not* always respected by the germ carriers.

Flowers, of course, have always been the principal source of perfume, although they are currently being overtaken by the chemist's flasks and test tubes. The earliest scents were more like unguents than anything else, and some of their recipes have survived. Among them is the formula for the old Egyptian perfume, Kyphi. No one knows just how old it is, but a list of its main ingredients found in the pyramid of Cheops mentioned juniper, sweet flag, cardamom, and myrrh. The Greeks, under the Ptolemies, later modified it, and Plutarch speaks of Kyphi as having some sixteen components, among them crocus, bdellium *(Acacia senegal),* and spikenard *(Nardostachys jatamansi).* Drying, powdering, sifting, soaking, and mixing took place in an elaborate process, and the final product was used as a fumigant, a perfume and in embalming.

The Egyptians had devised other unguents and perfumes, some of which were very costly. Oil of lily was greatly prized, as was Mendesium, made from myrrh, oil of ben *(Moringa oleifera,* also known as the Horseradish Tree because of the flavor of its roots), and canella, which was probably sugar cane, medieval nomenclature being as uncertain as it is. Another favorite scent was Metopium, a blend of almonds, honey, wine, resin, myrrh and sweet flag *(Acorus calamus),* and Cyprinum, a greenish tinted extract from henna flowers. Remnants of these perfumes have occasionally been accidentally sealed in

Roses invite noses to sniff for fragrance—look for bees before checking the aroma. Rose petals are often used in the making of perfume.

their containers, and found to retain faint traces of their original aroma even after some three thousand years. Although compounded in Egypt, the aromas generally owed more to the Greek and Roman rulers of that ancient world than to the heirs of the Pharaohs. Rome in particular cultivated vast tracts of roses in the delta region of the Nile, for use in the ceremonies and triumphs that took place in the imperial city so frequently at the time. Showers of fragrant rose petals and flowers would be lavished on the guests at Nero's banquets, sometimes even serving as funeral decorations shortly afterwards.

With the fall of Rome the Arab world moved into the forefront of discovery and development, thanks to the Arabs' possession of unaltered Greek texts, and their own centers of learning where knowledge was revered, preserved and discussed. They introduced the use of ambergris in order to delay the loss of fragrant volatile oils, and thus greatly extended the aromatic life of many of the perfumer's ingredients. The origin of this waxlike solid was long a mystery, assigned to sources as varied as submarine trees, fountains of the deep, and excretions of both fish and seabirds. Not until the whaling industry gained prominence was it recognized as an intestinal product of the whale.

The art of distillation, although known and practiced from ancient times, was greatly improved by the Arabic chemists. They devised the separate elements of the distilling apparatus, which consists of a retort, the portion holding the substance to be distilled, the condenser, which gathers and directs the vol-

atile vapors, and the receiver which holds the resultant fully condensed fluids. By exercising increased control throughout various stages of the process the distillers could separate out particular elements from highly complex mixtures, and then carefully analyze them. The complicated procedures of modern industrial chemistry all trace back to the early practices of the Arabic makers of perfume.

Attar of roses, although not a distillate, is somewhat akin to the process of distillation since it traps oils in fluid, and then floats them to the surface where they may be gathered with relative ease. The concentrated oil of roses was discovered accidentally by an Indian princess who noticed a film that had formed about some rose blossoms and petals lying in a pool. The princess was probably apocryphal, but the event was not; this phenomenon had more than likely been observed by palace servants long before the sensibilities of the royal nose ever came on the scene. The attar was produced in Persia, India, and in Bulgaria, which is its modern center of production, with vast tracts of roses being grown annually for the perfume trade, though synthetics have made inroads.

Throughout the medieval period Europe had little interest in maintaining a pleasant smell; unwashed linen and barnyard odors affronted the nose, but with the arrival of the Renaissance and the Elizabethan age matters took quite a turn for the better. Cloaks and gloves were scented, floors were rubbed with rosemary, while perfume shops opened their doors in Rome, Paris and London. Violets left aromatic trails on the air, carnations wafted their spicy smell indoors, orange blossoms offered new nasal delights, and once again the olfactory pleasures of Egypt, Greece, Rome, and Arabia were revived. Geranium oil became an important addition to the aromatic arsenal, especially as an adulterant of many of the rarer and more expensive oils. Lavender, from southern France and England, lent its clean, invigorating fragrance to linens, preserving them from the ravages of moths, and permeated the household with a most delightful scent, the very essence of domesticity. Jasmine, that delicate damosel from the Orient and the tropics, breathed forth its light, inimitable sweetness, floating on the air of moonlit, marble palaces, shimmering like the ghost of frangipani flowers.

Nearly a hundred separate volatile oils were derived from flowers, then blended into innumerable combinations. Neroli was drawn from the bitter orange, *Citrus aurantium,* while vetiver came from the tropical blossom, *Vetiveria zizanioides,* and orris root was powdered from the rhizomes of *Iris pallida* and *I. florentina.* Lemon grass came from *Cymbopogon citratus,* cassie from *Acacia farnesiana,* and ylang-ylang, the flower of flowers, was extracted from *Cananga odorata.* The latter has been known in the Occident only since 1864, but in little more than one hundred years it has become almost indispensable, entering into nearly every perfume made. And to the list of natural oils may be added the scent of new mown hay, coumarin, now produced synthetically, violet, made from the chemical ionone, vanilla, from wood pulp, and a host of others born of the coal-tar, pulp wood, and petroleum industries.

The lure of perfume has spawned an extensive trade and manufacture of scent, that has grown mightily since Marie de Medici established it at Grasse, France, some four hundred years ago. The floral oils, necessary to the modern perfumer, fall far short of the demand, hence the heavy reliance on synthetics. For example, it requires 30,000 pounds of violets to produce one pound of oil. In Bulgaria well over 12,000 acres of roses must be grown to satisfy that country's suppliers of attar of roses. Billions of flowers are grown for their precious essential oils alone, and it is no wonder that the perfume makers have had to search out, or invent, alternate sources of supply.

One method of extending the materials available has been by means of dilution. Beginning as early as 1370, with the appearance of Hungary water, the practice of making colognes became increasingly popular. The concoction consisted of oil of rosemary in 92% alcohol. Some centuries later such

With the arrival of the Renaissance came a renewed interest in fragrances. Lavender was used to add its clean aroma to linens and to preserve them from the ravages of moths.

"waters" gained the title of cologne because they were distributed from the city of that name. The sweet smelling water was made there by an emigrant Italian family, but it had to wait almost a century to become sought after, which it did once Napoleon's armies brought about its distribution throughout Europe. It was a truly international scent, having been formulated by the Italians, made in Germany, and popularized by the French. It contained the oils of rosemary, neroli, citron, and bergamot, steeped in three gallons of spirits of wine. Another favorite, once the monopoly of Tsars, was Russian leather, which was distilled from birch-tar oil derived from the wood and bark of the white birch, *Betula alba.*

Lately such a concept as a perfume center, as envisioned by Marie de Medici, seems to have vanished. All the great innovators of the past, Houbigant, Guerlain, and Coty have been replaced by chemists in white laboratory coats, working in concert with financiers from Tokyo, London, Los Angeles and Zurich. Their headquarters are linked by computers, which are apt to be "down" at any given and inopportune moment. Individual artistry has been strangled by "success," and technology is being subverted by an expanding scientific illiteracy. Nonetheless the sense of smell, generated from our genes and human capacities, will eventually prevail. Odors, like sweet, soft music dying/Keep the heart of memory asighing. Perfume, after all, is a blend of poetry and nature, having evocative powers that linger in the mind long after every trace of scent has gone. ❧

The Fragrant Flower Garden

Mary Ann McGourty

One of my most vivid memories of childhood, growing up on the coast of Virginia, is the sweet scent of gardenias that filled the early summer air. With the windows open to catch each welcome breeze, our house was filled day and night with the fragrance of the waxy white flowers. For many people fragrant plants are synonymous with old-fashioned plants, and they recall a time when the world and our own lives seemed less complicated. Perhaps that is part of their appeal.

Are "modern" plants less fragrant? In recent years hybridizers' efforts seem to be focused on creating plant varieties with larger flowers in a wider range of colors on hardier, more disease-resistant plants. While these new selections may be better in some ways than the old-timers, they are frequently less fragrant. It is certainly possible, however, to create a garden combining the best qualities of older plants with the improvements of the modern age.

Siting Scented Plants

The success of a fragrant garden depends as much on placement of the plants as it does on the choice of plants to include. You can situate

Mary Ann McGourty and her husband, Fred, are the owners of Hillside Gardens in Norfolk, Connecticut. Her articles have appeared in American Horticulturist *and the Brooklyn Botanic Garden handbooks* Perennials and their Uses *and* Gardening Under Lights. *She is the major contributor and editor of* Taylor's Guide to Ground Covers, Vines and Grasses *(Houghton Mifflin, 1987).*

"Fragrance, perhaps, speaks more clearly . . . to age than to youth. With the young it may not pass much beyond the olfactory nerve, but with those who have started down the far side of the hill it reaches into the heart."

The Fragrant Path
Louise Beebe Wilder

plants to take advantage of existing conditions, or you can create conditions that will take advantage of their fragrant quality. Whether you are siting trees, shrubs or herbaceous plants, consider the direction and intensity of the prevailing wind. If it is gentle, it will waft scents to you; if it is forceful, scents will dissipate before you can appreciate them. Where wind is frequently strong, create a sheltered area near a solid wall or an L of the house. Scents are often concentrated and enhanced by the warm, still air present in these protected locations.

A good site for fragrant plants (and others as well) is by a frequently used door or walkway. Not only can you enjoy the beauty and fragrance of the plants as you come and go, but you are likely to give more attention to the maintenance of plantings in such a prominent location. It is hard to overlook a flower gasping with dryness or one being crowded out by some gigantic weed.

A convenient location near a pathway is almost essential for enjoyment of the earliest bloomers in areas where spring is invariably preceded by mud season. Few of us are willing to tramp regularly across soggy lawns, leaving footprints as we go, or to get muddy knees as we view and sniff some early treasure.

Summer-flowering shrubs and herbaceous plants can be enjoyed from inside the house, as well as in the garden, if they are sited near a window that can be opened for soft breezes to enter. And a sunny location enhances the emission of essential oils responsible for the fragrance of flowers. Use caution, however, when placing heavily scented plants under a dining room window, as the senses of smell and taste are closely related, and it is possible to end up eating fish that tastes like roses. My childhood gardenias were a constant source of irritation to my father at mealtime, and we often ate dinner with the windows closed.

Some flowers are fragrant after dark. These can be enjoyed in a small border or in containers near a patio or porch where you sit to relax after a day's work. In fact, many people find that sweet scents have a calming effect — just what is needed at the end of a busy day. Be sure to include white flowers by the patio, as many of them are fragrant, and white is the last color to disappear into the darkness.

Raised beds are especially useful for displaying and enjoying low-growing plants, as it is possible to place the nose near the source of the fragrance without resorting to deep knee bends or other calisthenics. Many herbs are arranged in this manner, but raised beds can also be used to advantage for small bulbs.

Timing

There are two different approaches to fragrant gardens. Some people have a romantic notion of wandering into the garden, to be overwhelmed by the intermingling of many powerful scents. This can be akin to putting a tape cassette of Dixieland jazz on your stereo, while the radio is tuned to the Metropolitan Opera, and a friend plays his rendition of Chopin's "Minute Waltz" on your piano. Overwhelming, perhaps, but can you appreciate each component?

Another approach is to set each kind of scented plant apart from the others in the garden, so that you can enjoy the plants individually. Sweet woodruff (*Galium odoratum*) then, would not be used as a ground cover under fragrant lilacs (*Syringa*), which flower at the same time in May. Instead, plant under the lilacs lightly scented early snowdrops (*Galanthus*), followed by a fragrant annual that begins flowering later; then use sweet woodruff under the early *Viburnum carlesii* or August-flowering summersweet (*Clethra alnifolia*). The most effective gardens (fragrance or otherwise) are those that provide a sequence of interest, whether the attraction comes from flowers, leaves or fruit. There is always something to look forward to as the season progresses.

The plants chosen for any garden are a matter of personal preference. People like different scents, and individuals perceive fragrances differently. One person may like the heavy, sweet smell of mock-orange (*Philadelphus*), while another prefers the clean, lemony scent of magnolias and finds the mock-orange cloying and overpowering. The point is, include in your garden the fragrant plants that appeal to you.

How can you tell in advance which plants are fragrant? Sometimes there is a clue in the name, such as honeysuckle, sweet autumn clematis, *Myrrhis odorata* or *Osmanthus fragrans*. Also look for plants whose flowers have single rows of petals or that are naturally double. Those whose petals have been doubled by hybridization frequently lack fragrance, as the extra petals replace the plants' oil-bearing reproductive parts. This is the reason many of the showiest flowering crabapples and cherries lack fragrance and also do not set fruit.

Shrubs, vines, perennials, bulbs, herbs and annuals all have a place in the fragrant garden. We will look at a few perennials and bulbs here, as the other types of plants are covered elsewhere in this volume.

Scented Perennial Flowers

Among the old-fashioned flowers, peonies immediately come to mind. These come in a profusion of forms and colors, but many are not fragrant, or only slightly so. If in doubt,

Cimifuga racemosa *and* Phlox *'Sir John Falstaff* *complement one another and add fragrance to* *the garden. When planting for fragrance,* *consider the direction of the prevailing breezes* *which can waft scent to your open windows,* *porch or deck.*

choose peonies while they are in bloom. Most fragrant are the pink and white varieties derived from *Paeonia lactiflora,* such as 'Mrs. Franklin Roosevelt' or 'Sarah Bernhardt' (both deep pink). 'Duchesse de Nemours' is a good white, and 'Festiva Maxima' is white with red flecks. They are the latest to bloom in June and the longest in flower, but the large heads frequently topple after a heavy rain. Plant peonies in full sun in rich, well-drained soil with the "eyes" one to two inches below the soil level. Most grow two-and-one-half to three-feet high at maturity and will not require division for many years.

Another old-timer is red-valerian or Jupiter's beard (*Centranthus ruber*). It carries deep pinkish-red flowers on two-to-three foot stems in early summer, and there is also a white-flowered form. Because of its sometimes uneven growth habit, it will benefit from a moderate shearing after the first wave of flowers and will reward the tidy gardener with more flowers in late summer. It prefers a

slightly higher soil pH than many perennials, so work a small amount of dolomitic limestone into the soil at planting time.

The border pinks (*Dianthus plumarius*) and border carnations (*D. caryophyllus*) with their mats of silvery foliage, are good front-of-the-border plants, provided drainage is excellent; but they will soon rot out in heavy soils where water collects. The spice-scented flowers on one-foot-tall stems are pink, white, red or bicolor in early summer. They prefer a loose soil in full sun and will also benefit from a little lime.

Cat valerian or garden heliotrope (*Valeriana officinalis*) has clusters of white flowers on four-to-five foot stems in June. The finely cut leaves are attractive throughout the season if plants are cut back halfway after flowering. This vigorous plant is fragrant day and night and will tolerate extra soil moisture without sulking. As the common name suggests, cats are occasionally attracted to the plant, and they can maul it as they do catnip, though our own cats are only mildly interested. A few thorny barberry twigs stuck into the ground around valerian should solve the problem if your cat is hooked.

A plant worth seeking out is *Dictamnus albus,* the gas plant. Its flowers and leaves smell of lemons on a hot day when the sun draws its volatile oils into the air. Its taproot makes gas plant difficult to transplant successfully except when young. Spikes of pink or white flowers appear on two-to-three foot stems in late spring or early summer.

A mainstay of the mid-season garden is summer phlox (*P. paniculata*). Several white-flowered cultivars are fragrant, including 'World Peace' and 'White Admiral', both blooming in August and September on three-foot tall plants. A personal favorite is 'Sir John Falstaff', which is a clear salmon-pink in July. Summer phlox grows best in moisture-retentive soil in a sunny location, but it will still flower well in light shade. Powdery mildew, which frequently mars the leaves, can be controlled by regular applications of Benlate, a systemic fungicide, beginning in late spring. New *Phlox maculata* 'Alpha' (mauve-pink)

Masses of Narcissus poeticus *bloom at Brooklyn Botanic Garden. They are very fragrant.*

and 'Omega' (white with a pink eye) are reputedly less susceptible to mildew, though we have seen it thrive on them in shaded areas where air circulation is poor. Each has shiny lance-shaped leaves and bears flowers in cone-shaped heads instead of rounded clusters. They bloom in June with repeats in late summer if deadheaded promptly after the first wave of flowers. The all-white bedding phlox, 'Miss Lingard', a popular old-timer, is now usually included in this species. For the spring woodland garden, wood phlox (*P. divaricata*)

Hemerocallis 'Hyperion' blooms in July and is one of the few hybrid daylilies with discernible fragrance.

and creeping *P. stolonifera* are fragrant, low-growing ground covers in white or blue. *P. stolonifera* also comes in a good pink color form, 'Pink Ridge', as well as a deep purple.

For the shaded spring garden, consider primulas, especially the English primrose (*P. vulgaris*). The species has single light yellow flowers on six-inch tall stems over clumps of basal leaves. The new Barnhaven strain includes several lovely pastel shades, as well as some with double flowers. Primroses maintain their vigor well if divided every second or third year and planted in moist, humusy soil. The cowslip (*P. veris*) and polyanthus (*P. x polyantha*) are also lightly fragrant and thrive under the same cultural conditions.

Sweet violets (*Viola odorata*) naturalize well in the high shade of deciduous trees, but they are frequently too spotty to make a dense ground cover. They will put forth a good flush of flowers in early spring and again in the autumn if they are well fertilized in soil that is not too acid. Some popular selections are 'Royal Robe' (purple), 'Red Giant' (deep red) and 'White Czar'. Try interplanting them with daffodils for a spring sensory tonic.

Daylilies (*Hemerocallis*) are not usually associated with fragrance, but several less well-known species, including the lemon or

flava daylily (*H. lilioasphodelus*) have scent. One of the earliest to bloom, the lemon daylily, bears small yellow flowers on three-foot scapes in late May or June. This is followed in July by yellow 'Hyperion', one of the few hybrid daylilies with discernible fragrance. What a pity that hybridizers have tended to ignore the fragrant species when breeding for larger flowers and more frills.

Hostas are stalwarts of the shaded garden, but few have fragrant flowers. 'Royal Standard', 'Honeybells' and one of their parents, *H. plantaginea,* are valuable for their scented flowers in August, when many gardens are looking a bit down at the heels. The white pearl buds of 'Royal Standard' and *H. plantaginea* open into pure white trumpets held over clumps of spreading, shiny green leaves. 'Honeybells' is similar, with pale lavender flowers. Hostas are effective ground covers, and because most break dormancy late in spring, they are useful in hiding the yellowed foliage of early bulbs planted nearby.

Fragrant Foliage, Too
Some plants, including many culinary and ornamental herbs and also a few traditional garden perennials have the bonus of scented leaves as well as flowers. All parts of bee balm (*Monarda didyma*) smell of mint and oranges. Like many members of the mint family, it can spread rapidly from the root and become a garden menace if planted in moist soil in a sunny location. Control its takeover tendencies by planting a few sprigs in a bucket with drainage holes, which is then sunk into the ground up to its rim. The red-flowered bee balms, including the three-foot tall 'Cambridge Scarlet' and 'Adam', are the most vigorous, and they are prime attractors of hummingbirds. 'Prairie Night' and 'Blue Stocking' are somewhat taller and more maroon in color; 'Croftway Pink', a pastel three-footer, is less aggressive.

Autumn chrysanthemums (*C.* x *morifolium*) and feverfew (*C. parthenium*) have a pungency of flower and leaf that not everyone appreciates. Autumn mums come in many flower forms and all colors except blue. The

low-growing, small-flowered cushion sorts seem to be the hardiest, and their longevity will increase if they are planted where soil drainage is excellent. Chrysanthemums benefit from adequate water and several light applications of a balanced fertilizer during the growing season. They flower best in full sun, although feverfew flowers well in light shade over a long period, beginning in June. You can control lanky growth of mums by pinching out the growing tips several times early in the season.

Many silver-leaf plants, including some artemisias and achilleas, have aromatic foliage. These dry-landers are at their best in full sun in light, sandy soil that drains well. Their silver or gray-green leaves add a welcome contrast to green foliage in the sunny garden. Southernwood (*Artemisia abrotanum*) grows three- to four-feet tall and is shrubby. Prune it back in early spring to maintain a compact growth habit. *A. ludoviciana* 'Silver King' and 'Silver Queen' have upright, three-foot stems that are handsome in dried arrangements or wreaths. The latter cultivar has slightly wider leaf blades, and, is thus somewhat showier. Both will romp if let loose in the garden, a situation easily controlled by a sunken bucket straitjacket. For the front of the border silver mound artemisia (*A. schmidtiana*) is choice, as its soft, silvery bottlebrush foliage catches light and reflects it. If clumps look shabby and open up in late summer, trim them back part way.

The golden yarrows, including hybrid *Achillea* 'Coronation Gold' (three-feet tall) and 'Moonshine' (two feet) have flat heads of yellow flowers held on strong stems over clumps of pungent, silvery, finely cut foliage.

These and other plants with aromatic foliage have other good qualities too. They seem to have fewer insect problems than other plants and are less often browsed by deer, who apparently do not like the strong taste of the leaves. Fragrance is most pronounced when the leaves are bruised or crushed; place aromatic plants by a walkway or door, so you can touch them as you pass by.

A Few Bulbs

Many spring and summer bulbs have a faint earthy scent if we bury our noses in their flowers, but a few are notable for their sweet aroma. Among fragrant daffodils the small- and medium-flowered kinds predominate; most have two to five flowers per stem. *Narcissus jonquilla* hybrids and selections, including 'Lintie', 'Suzy' and 'Trevithian', prefer a sandy soil that dries out in summer. *N. tazetta* types are very fragrant, but many are not reliably hardy in the North. 'Cheerfulness', 'Canarybird' and 'Geranium' are worth a try. Late-flowering *N. poeticus,* the old pheasant's eye, including 'Actaea', is good for naturalizing and will tolerate some moisture. Grow daffodils in full sun or in the shade of deciduous trees. They should thrive undisturbed for years if planted in well-drained, root-free soil and fertilized annually as the leaves emerge.

All varieties of spring hyacinth (*Hyacinthus orientalis*) are fragrant and reasonably winter hardy, but they have a stiff, formal appearance in the garden. This effect can be softened by allowing them to come up through a loose ground cover such as vinca or sweet woodruff.

Lilium regale, the regal lily, is regal indeed. In July its large white trumpets on five-to-six-foot stems dominate the garden and perfume the air day and night. Regal lilies have no basal foliage, so group them in the center or rear of the border where shorter plants will hide the lilies' leggy stems. Aurelian hybrid lilies such as 'Black Dragon', 'Pink Perfection' and 'Golden Splendor' are similar in bloom time and appearance. Shorter (three to four feet) Oriental hybrids with recurved petals extend the fragrant lilies into August and September. Pink-flowered 'Uchida' and pure white 'Arctic Treasure' are deservedly popular; provide a skirt of foliage for them too. Lilies grow best in rich, well-drained soil. Some prefer full sun, but many benefit from light afternoon shade, which keeps their colors from fading.

There is a wealth of other fragrant plants for experimentation. By the careful choice and placement of perennials and other scented plants, the gardener can easily have a garden of interest from spring until fall, one that appeals to the nose as well as to the eye. ❧

Bibliography

Damrosch, Barbara. *Theme Gardens,* New York: Workman Publishing, 1982.

Rohde, Eleanour Sinclair. *The Scented Garden,* London: The Medici Society, 1931. (Reprint), Detroit: Gale Research Co., 1974.

Taylor, Norman. *Fragrance in the Garden,* New York: D. Van Nostrand Co., 1953.

Verey, Rosemary. *The Scented Garden,* New York: Van Nostrand Reinhold Co., 1981.

Wilder, Louise Beebe. *The Fragrant Path,* New York: MacMillan Co., 1932. Reprinted as *The Fragrant Garden,* New York: Dover Publications, 1974.

Wilson, Helen VanPelt and Bell, Leonie. *The Fragrant Year,* New York: M. Barrows & Co., 1967.

Sources for Fragrant Perennials

Bluestone Perennials, Inc. 7211 Middle Ridge Rd., Madison, OH 44057

Daffodil Mart, Rte. 3, Box 794, Gloucester, VA 23061

Far North Gardens, 16785 Harrison, Livonia, MI 48154 (seeds, including Barnhaven primroses)

Fragrant Path, P.O. Box 328, Fort Calhoun, NE 68023 (seeds)

Hillside Gardens, 515 Litchfield Rd., Norfolk, CT 06058 (no shipping)

Holbrook Farm & Nursery, Rte. 2, Box 223B, Fletcher, NC 28732

Van Bourgondien Bros., P.O. Box A, 245 Farmingdale Rd., Babylon, NY 11702 (bulbs)

Wayside Gardens, Hodges, SC 29695

White Flower Farm, P.O. Box 50, Litchfield, CT 06759

Fragrant Annuals

. . . the sowing of a seed seems a very simple matter, but I always feel as if it were a sacred thing among the mysteries of God. Standing by that space of blank and motionless ground, I think of all it holds for me of beauty and delight, and I am filled with joy at the thought that I may be the magician to whom power is given to summon so sweet a pageant from the silent and passive soil.

—Celia Thaxter

Edward R. Rasmussen

The number of significantly scented annuals is not so great that most of them cannot be mentioned in an article of this scope. For the same reason, a garden of moderate size could accommodate them all in the space of a season or two. It is a pleasant task to decide which to plant.

Many people think of annuals as temporary fillers to be used until perennials can take their place. Others, preferring to start with a

Edward R. Rasmussen is proprietor of The Fragrant Path in Calhoun, Nebraska, which specializes in seeds for fragrant, rare, and old-fashioned plants. He is curator of the Norwood Arboretum in Omaha, Nebraska.

Trumpet vine trained into a standard with a peony at its base.

clean palette each season, sow only annuals. The most colorful and interesting garden combines both. Perennials furnish a framework and sense of continuity, while annuals offer an extended blooming season and some of the brightest, most colorful flowers. New annuals can always be tried next year.

This list of fragrant annuals begins with *Artemisia annua* which is commonly known as sweet Annie or sweet wormwood. It is a tall, rank-growing plant that might be used as a summer hedge in place of kochia as it serves the same purpose with the bonus of fragrant foliage that can be used for wreaths when the season is over. Lacy as any fern, it is good as a foil in the border and to cut for filler in arrangements.

The sweet sultans, *Centaurea imperialis* and *C. moschata*, are quite fragrant and such serviceable plants that any garden will benefit from their presence. They flower all summer in white, yellow, and shades of pink-through-

Iris germanica and Cheiranthus cheiri *make a dramatic combination. Wallflower is among the most fragrant of plants—it does not like hot weather, but is worth a try.*

purple on long stems that are good for cutting. Tolerant of poor soil and drought, they grow to about three feet in average conditions. Native to the Middle East, their common name is derived from the Sultan of Turkey who had a great affection for them.

A biennial in most of its forms, the wallflower, *Cheiranthus cheiri*, grows best in the British Isles and the Pacific Northwest—hot summers are not to its liking. Still, along with its relatives dame's rocket and common stock, it is among the most fragrant of plants, so it is worth some effort to have. In Parkinson's time it was so valued for its sweetness that it was a likely constituent of any nosegay—thus its Latin name, which means 'handflower'. Fortunately for those of us who live in climates too cold for it to overwinter, there are such annual strains as 'Paris Market' and 'Early Wonder'. If started early these can bloom before the weather gets too hot—or failing that, they can wait until summer's heat is gone.

A curiosity that is seldom seen today is Queen Anne's pocket melon, *Cucumis melo dudaim*, also known as sweet-scented or pomegranate melon. The inedible fruit is so small it can be tucked into the purse or pocket for use in confronting foetors and effluvia. Vilmorin-Andrieux says it is used as an ornamental climber on trellises and arbors.

To add a tropical feeling to the garden or veranda, the daturas, with their luxuriant foliage and great trumpet-shaped flowers, might be worth considering. Those worth growing for annual decoration come mainly from the species *Datura metel*. The flowers are commonly white, yellow or purple and single or trumpet-in-trumpet in form. Start them early indoors, as you would tomatoes, for a longer blooming season, or grow in a pot as a specimen. They are highly fragrant at night. All parts of the plant are poisonous.

The *Dianthus* tribe offers many and varied fragrances, but unfortunately the annual sorts are not fragrant. So associated are *Dianthus* (the Latin name means flower of the Gods) with rich and spicy odors, that one can hardly help be disappointed when, upon raising one to the nose, it is found to be mute. If you wish

25

Dianthus superbus

ornamental seedpods. This climber does not get leggy at the base as many others do.

Another odorous, robust clamberer is the mock cucumber, *Echinocystis lobata*, native to the eastern half of North America. It is useful for screening and covering unsightly objects since under favorable conditions its growth is very rapid—up to thirty feet in a single season. If the prickly pods are cut before they mature, they make very curious and interesting material for drying. Celia Thaxter describes the "large, loose clusters of starry white flowers" as "having a pure, delicious fragrance like honey and the wax of the comb."

A third member of this exclusive group of twining odorous plants, and also a rapid grower, is the moonflower, *Ipomoea alba*. Its white six-inch trumpets open in the evening and diffuse a powerful clovelike perfume—the flowers open rather quickly and can be interesting to watch. As with other ipomoeas, this vine should not be planted in too rich a soil or will run to rank growth with few flowers. If planted in a place where the morning sun doesn't reach it, the flowers may stay open longer.

Nearly everyone is familiar with the sweet pea, *Lathyrus odoratus*. Hundreds of varieties have been used since it came to the florists' attention in 1870, and more are coming. The old grandiflora varieties seem the most fragrant. They are also more tolerant of adverse growing conditions than many of the more recently developed strains. If you wish to grow the larger, fancier types and have the conditions to suit them, then look for those that are noted for their fragrance in the catalog descriptions.

Nasturtium, *Tropaeolum majus*, is not often thought of as a climber. However, some of the taller varieties can reach eight feet and with a little training make a very showy and effective screen. The common name means nose-turning" and refers to the pungently scented foliage, but the flowers are often sweetly fragrant too, many times with a pungent undertone. Plant in full sun and soil that is not too rich. If they are growing rankly

your annual pinks to speak, there are several that might be tried. The scentless Chinese pinks crossed with the carnation have given us a fragrant race called Marguerite carnations. Sown at any time, they will bloom in five months and continue until frost. 'Dwarf Fragrance' is a shorter version, and 'Sweet Wivelsfield' is a different cross that can be similarly treated. One of the most redolent of the lot is *Dianthus superbus*—I have detected its perfume from up to thirty yards away on a calm evening. It is normally a biennial to perennial, but if started early enough it will make a showing the first fall before exhausting itself the following summer.

The hyacinth bean, *Dolichos lablab*, has a delicate scent difficult to describe. Its fragrance is very similar to that of the grass *Sporobolus heterolepis*, prairie dropseed. Hyacinth bean has either white or purple flowers that are good to cut; if left to mature they form at the expense of bloom, sometimes pinching off some of the leaves will throw them into blossom.

White-flowered gourds, *Lagenaria siceraria*, which are the larger gourds, make interesting vigorous climbers, and their large white flowers are fragrant. Also, some other plants that we may not think of as being scented, if caught at the right time and condition, may be significantly perfumed. One morning a visitor to the garden walked up to a morning-glory (*Ipomoea tricolor* 'Blue Star') for what I thought would be a nuzzle with disappointment, but she exclaimed "old-ladies face powder" and upon inspection I had to concur.

A strongly scented annual that is seldom seen is Moldavian balm or dragonhead, *Dracocephalum moldavica*, which has gray-green foliage and lavender-blue flowers in long spikes for most of the summer. Quite hardy, and growing to about a foot and a half, it is easily raised from seed directly sown. Both the foliage and flowers smell of lemon and the plant is very attractive to bees and butterflies.

Erysimum asperum, known as the Siberian wallflower, must derive its name for its very hardy nature, for it is native from Ohio to the Rocky Mountains. Generally a biennial, it can easily be used as an annual if sown early. Related to the true wallflower, *Cheiranthus cheiri*, *Erysimum* might be a better candidate for areas too hot and too cold for the former. The scent, a combination of clove and lily, is similar as well.

Nicotiana alata

Heliotrope, fondly known as cherry-pie plant, *Heliotropium arborescens* (*H. peruvianum*), is a useful plant from Peru. It is actually a perennial, but is often used for summer bedding, tub plantings, hanging baskets and standards. It cannot tolerate any frost, so it must not be set out too early. There are dwarf strains with deep purple flowers, but these have little scent—the paler flowered taller strains seem to be the most fragrant with an almond-vanilla scent.

A familiar and much used edging and carpeting plant whose flowers have the refreshing aroma of newly mown hay is *Lobularia maritima* (often still listed as *Alyssum maritimum*, the ubiquitous sweet alyssum. Do not expect much in the way of sweetness from the colored varieties, for they have very little. Most of the white varieties still have good fragrance—especially the type plant— and 'Little Dorrit' and 'Carpet of Snow' are two good dwarf variations.

Pineapple weed, *Matricaria matricarioides*, is a little plant of scant ornamental value that grows in inhospitable waste places and disappears by midsummer. It is nice to have in walkways as it is carefree and is quite fragrant when trodden upon. In California it is known as manzanilla. A fine tisane is made from the leaves and flower heads as well.

There are two species of *Matthiola* that belong in every fragrant garden: *M. longipetala* (formerly *M. bicornus*), evening stock; and *M. incana*, common stock. The former might be mistaken for a weed for it is a rather forlorn looking. But at night its sweet, searching scent makes it desirable. Sow it along a path or under a window where its fragrance may be enjoyed.

Common stock is available in many forms and colors—the double-flowered forms are most fragrant. Whole villages of the weavers of Saxony were once devoted to raising stocks—and only one color was permitted to be grown per village to keep the strains pure. There are both annual and biennial types and ones for different seasons of the year, so be sure to choose with this in mind.

A denizen of many an old-fashioned garden, the marvel of Peru, *Mirabilis jalapa*, can be dug in the fall and stored like a dahlia. However, it comes so quickly from seed that it is nearly always treated as an annual. The flowers smell of citrus and may be yellow, crimson, pink, white, or various combinations of these; if you find one you particularly like you may wish to store the tuber. The flowers open in the late afternoon giving rise to its other common name, four o'clock. The blossoms also attract the hummingbird moth.

Another genus much favored for evening fragrance is *Nicotiana*, ornamental tobacco. The most common of the three species considered here is probably *N. alata*, jasmine-tobacco. There are now many dwarf forms in various colors, but they have little fragrance compared to the tall night-flowered parent. It is not much to look at during the day, but it is worth having for its wonderful scent.

Nicotiana suaveolens, a sweet-scented native of Australia, is one of the only tobaccos not indigenous to the Americas. As it is of shorter stature and finer texture than most it is of more value to those who don't have room for the larger *N. sylvestris*, woodland tobacco. This floral giant can reach six feet in a season and makes a novel accent in a group of three. The freesia-scented flowers are borne in panicles at the top of the plant but droop down, making sniffing easier—though it isn't really necessary as it is free with its fragrance.

Although I don't intend to deal with the annual herbs, I might mention that purple-leaved basil has value in the border for its colored foliage and flower spikes. Holy basil, *Ocimum sanctum*, is also very fragrant, and the stem base is cut into beads for rosaries by Hindus who plant it about temple gardens. Allowed to mature their spikes of seed clusters make good material for fragrant dried arrangements, or for tying in bundles to be tossed on the coals of a fire.

Since there are so many varieties of petunia and their ranks are always changing, shop by smelling the flowers for fragrance. The best scents are found in the purple and white types, and they are usually most perfumed at night.

One plant which likely would never have received the attentions of the florist were it not for its distinctive and powerful fragrance is mignonette, *Reseda odorata*. Napoleon encountered it as a little weed in North Africa and sent seed to the Empress Josephine. It subsequently was named Mignonette, 'little darling', by the French. It is very nice to have along a path or near a dooryard or patio or in a pot where its perfume can drift. Some of the more modern varieties are not as fragrant as the less developed sorts. A similar scent comes from the vineyard when certain varieties of grape are in bloom—some describe it as grapeflower and sweetpeas—an intoxicating combination indeed.

Scabiosa atropurpurea, known as sweet scabious, pincushion flower and mourning

Nicotiana sylvestris, *woodland tobacco, is one of the plants noted for its evening fragrance. This one can reach six feet in height.*

Lobularia maritima, *sweet alyssum, is often used as edging and carpeting plants and lends the aroma of newly mown hay to the air. Here it is combined with parsley, verbena and* sempervivum.

brilliant single flowers. Roy Genders considers its foliage "... more refreshingly aromatic than of any other plant, the lemon verbenalike perfume remaining on the fingers for an hour or more after pressing the leaves." Some varieties to look for are: 'Golden Gem', 'Lemon Gem' and 'Paprika'.

Schizopetalon walkeri is a delicate small annual from Chile. It doesn't have a common name. The feathery pure white flowers are powerfully almond scented. It resents root disturbance and must be directly sown, or started and kept in pots. I once saw it described as easy, but I have yet to succeed in flowering it, though I have tried several times. I have a few seeds left and I think I'll probably give it another try this spring. ॐ

bride (for the somber color of the original type) has long been a popular flower for garden decoration and for cutting. A plant of open fields, it needs an open, sunny position in the garden. It is available in many colors, but the purple-black and sky-blue are the most richly scented.

A plant that possesses the scent of lily-of-the-valley is the wind poppy, *Stylomecon heterophylla*. Growing to no more than two feet, it can be given poppy culture but with a little shade. The flowers are brick-red with a dark eye and are good for cutting if treated like Iceland poppies.

Some think of the marigold as a fragrant plant and some consider it merely malodorous. But the signet marigold, *Tagetes tenuifolia* 'Pumila', has a scent that can be appreciated. It is less than a foot high with finely incised foliage covered in masses of

Bibliography

Coon, Nelson. *Gardening for Fragrance Indoors and Out*. New York: Hearthside Press, 1970.

Genders, Roy. *Scented Flora of the World*. New York: St. Martin's Press, 1977.

Loewer, Peter. *The Annual Garden*. Emmaus, PA: Rodale Press, 1988.

Thaxter, Celia. *An Island Garden*. Boston: Houghton Mifflin Co., 1988.

Verey, Rosemary. *The Scented Garden*. New York: Van Nostrand Reinhold Co., 1981.

Wilder, Louise Beebe. *The Fragrant Garden*. New York: Dover Publications, Inc., 1974.

Wilson, Helen Van Pelt & Leonie Bell. *The Fragrant Year*. New York: Bonanza Books, 1967.

Sources

The Fragrant Path, P.O. Box 328, Fort Calhoun, NE 68023. Seeds.

Thompson & Morgan, P.O. Box 1308, Jackson, NJ 08527. Seeds.

Degiorgi Seed Co., 1529 North Saddle Creek Rd., Omaha, NE 68104. Seeds.

J.L. Hudson, Seedsman, P.O. Box 1058, Redwood City, CA 94064.

*Turf seat: The Holy Family with Three Hares.
Albrecht Dürer (1471-1528). The Metropolitan
Museum of Art, Gift of Junius S. Morgan, 1919
(19.73.168)*

Landscaping with Fragrant Herbs

James Adams

I n every garden there should be at least one place inhabited by temptations that lure noses and entice fingers. It may be an entranceway with fragrant herbs hugging a gate; scented creepers frolicking between stepping stones; tapestries of spicy herbs spilling from perches; a lush counterfeit lawn, an herbal carpet awaiting the soles of the venturesome; or here and there a bench or chair, an invitation to relax on a seat that is itself a garden—a living, fragrant turf seat.

Each of these commonplace components of the landscape—entrance, pathway, wall, lawn and seat—can be made memorable, and fragrant herbs are perfect for the task.

"Basil, Rocket, Valerian, Rue,

(Almost singing themselves they run),

Vervain, Dittany, Call-me-to-you—

Cowslip, Melilot, Rose-of-the-Sun"

These are some of the herbs that inspired Kipling. They are but a handful of the hundreds of fragrant treasures we may plant in our gardens.

Let's begin with the most celebrated of all, the jasmines and roses. Within these two remarkable groups are the twining, twisting, and climbing herbs that decorate and scent simultaneously and bear sweet-smelling flowers for lengthy periods if pruned and pampered. The very best of the jasmines are the evergreen Arabian (Zone 7-10) and the hardier 'Revolution' and poet's jasmine (Zone 6-10). Many trailing and climbing roses are hardy in the north. The memorial rose spreads

James Adams, a freelance writer who lives in Washington, is the author of Landscaping With Herbs *(Timber Press, 1987). He enjoys growing his own herbs and cooking for his wife and five children.*

quickly and is evergreen in warmer climates, while the chestnut rose is tolerant of poor soil and salty sea breezes and exceptional for smothering gates and fences.

These and other fragrant vines, including varieties of honeysuckle, grape, yam, and passiflora, are valuable for cloaking an arbor; clambering over archways and up trellises; espaliered on walls; gamboling over mounds of stone; or charmingly overpowering a gate. Use them alone or in sympathy with other colorful ornamental vines to provide fragrant air anywhere.

Jasmine, passion flower, and cinnamon vine (Chinese yam) adapt to containers that can be moved about in the garden to entertain guests wherever they roam. These vigorous climbers need heavy pruning to ensure a full crop of fragrant flowers. Don't forget the ordinary grape—the mouth-watering odor of sun-ripened concord grapes is memorable.

Three bushy evergreens that add grace and fragrance to the entranceway are lavender, rosemary and southernwood. These herbs can be pruned and shaped as desired, conforming to most demands in any landscape—formal or contemporary. They are equally suited to growing informally about a small bench.

Lavender's legendary essence is borne predominantly by the flowers, and it is reminiscent of the fine bath salts and delicate perfumes that rely on it as a main ingredient. Although the foliage is fragrant when handled, lavender is at its peak as flowers begin to open. Several plants can scent an entire yard. The lavenders come in many costumes. The cultivars 'Hidcote', 'Munstead', the pink-flowering 'Rosea', and the dwarf lavender

Photos by James Adams

'Nana' have the best shapes and respond to pruning. Grow lavender in coarse, sandy, limed soil surrounded by a one-inch layer of sand. Do not overwater.

Southernwood, a relative of the bitter, medicinally scented wormwood, is semi-evergreen, losing much of its foliage and fragrance during the winter. The cultivar 'Camphor' retains its aroma, however, and remains evergreen to about Zone 6. Use all the southernwoods, particularly those with a citrus scent, on corners where paths intersect so that their soft, feathery branches will be brushed by passers-by, leaving their clothing smelling sweetly of pine and lemon.

Rosemary is another pine-scented herb whose fragrance is remarkably perfumelike and is a popular ingredient in herbal hair and bath products. In the garden rosemary can be used in many ways. The upright varieties, which include white-flowering, pine-scented, 'Tuscan Blue' and 'Majorca Pink', can be used to create exceptionally fragrant hedges that can grow from four-to-six feet high and wide. Rosemary hedges work well encircling a bench or patio. They are commonly used as fragrant screens enclosing private niches in the landscape. A stroll through a rosemary hedge en route to a hidden garden is a special treat when in full bloom.

The creeping varieties of rosemary, including 'Huntington Carpet' and 'Lockwood de Forest', are more versatile and may be substituted for junipers. They can be used along

The author's garden contains a large rosemary on the left plus a potpourri of violets, monarda, oregano and cardoon.

entranceways or allowed to fall from ledges and elevated containers. Always arrange them so that their branches extend well into pathways where they will be brushed and bruised.

Creeping rosemary is especially suited for use in the fragrant bench—a large, raised container that has a seat surrounding the whole. Center plantings in an 18 to 24 inch-wide bed (9 to 12 inches from seat) and allow at least 12 to 18 inches between neighboring plants. Train the rosemary to spill outward over the bench. On a fragrant bench one sits beside, not on, the herbs. Always provide spaces on the bench for unobstructed sitting. Use a winter-flowering rosemary in warmer climates, or an evergreen lavender or creeping savory in colder areas. For a treat use the herbaceous Persian catnip, which has a clovelike scent.

An herb that works well in pathways is creeping thyme. There are many varieties; some of the most useful form dense carpets only one-quarter-to-four inches thick. Although they must be stepped on to release their odors, a crop of flowers of 20 or more will perfume your garden.

The thicker mats of caraway thyme, 'Clear Gold' thyme, the true Mother of Thymes, 'Fosterflower', and the lemon-scented 'White Magic', should be encouraged to grow into the path and to be trampled by passers-by. Other

A collection of lavender, spearmint, monarda, California poppies, lamb's ears and achillea make a colorful tapestry in this garden of mixed herbs and perennials.

The thinnest mats of creeping thyme include the gold-flecked 'Mayfair', 'White Moss', 'Tuffeted', and the wild thymes, 'Pink Chintz', crimson and woolly. A hot, midsummer sun will bake the fragrances of all of these thymes together into a delicious potpourri in your garden. Be sure to provide a corridor in which they can be spread between paving stones. Allow a space one-to-two inches wide and two inches deep. Let them establish themselves and then begin to prune or mow to remove damaged branches. Do not be afraid to force them lower and lower into a more resilient mat. Give them every opportunity to bloom, but otherwise mow them as often as you do your lawn, setting the mower to a height that just keeps them neat.

Some of the bush thymes, such as French, 'Orange Balsam' and the golden 'Doone Valley' can be used on embankments that contain narrow trails. There they can be brushed by pants cuffs and skirts but not stepped on. Prune them back a few inches to expose new growth after their flowers have turned brown. Thick banks of bush thymes may be used to encircle a sunken patio.

mat-forming, but less resilient thymes include the golden lemon, silver, and English. Display them beside the path to contribute fragrance from their flowers or from fondling by inquisitive hands.

Lavenders flank the walkway in the Adams' Washington State garden. Lavender's fragrance comes mostly from the flowers, but the leaves are also fragrant when brushed.

Two mints that are tops for carpeting a pathway are English pennyroyal and Corsican mint. Pennyroyal's value lies in its preference for the middle of the path where it spreads, oblivious to busy feet. In this situation a gardener can't be particular about appearance

for it is a sweet-smelling herb asking to be crushed.

Corsican mint is simply astonishing. Growing between paving stones or along fissures in a rock wall this diminutive mint packs one great minty wallop if bruised. Bricks with planted holes create an interesting pattern when Corsican mint peeks up at you from a multitude of green eyes. Full sun plenty of moisture and foot traffic are necessary. Without wear and tear it would overgrow, become spongy and less hardy. Constant traffic ensures a firm, healthy ground cover no thicker than one-quarter inch. It is not evergreen in colder climes but it will do well to Zone 6.

'Trenague' camomile is flowerless and grows slowly into a cushion that is so soft it beckons to be touched. Roman camomile, the flowering form, is more hardy and may be substituted, but it is not nearly as compact in habit, and its flowers require frequent pruning. Unhindered, 'Trenague' camomile forms lush, mossy tuffets, so if you want it for a pathway remember the camomile rule: 'A camomile bed, the more it is trodden, the more it will spread.'

Planted in a pathway, where it will constantly nurture weary feet, camomile will become a compact mat no thicker than one inch. Provide full sun, plenty of moisture, and an easy way for it to thread the maze of paving cracks, and this apple-scented herb will become a carpet.

Before we go on to other herbs, let's consider a turf seat of camomile. The turf seat is essentially a container with a fragrant herb doubling as a seat cover. The turf seat dates from antiquity. Amphitheaters, for sports or community activities, encircled by 'turf bleachers' are the earliest documented. They were simple to construct, cooler than stone, and cleaner than bare soil. Native meadow grasses were used as the living cover, and mowing was done by goats and sheep.

Gardeners in the Dark and Medieval Ages, inspired by the stale air within a castle's walls, employed turf seats to entertain and comfort. A mound of earth was pushed up, flattened, and planted with fragrant meadow plants or imported herbs that saturated the air with a richness. By the Middle Ages turf seats had grown in favor and been given form with brick and stone. They often stood alone, sentinels to many a knot garden, a spot to sit and reflect upon some gardener's handiwork. Garden seats everywhere came to be dressed with scented herbs because they afforded so remarkable an experience for so little effort. "Like the Temple Gardens at Thessaly, raised with gravel and sand, having seats and banks of camomile; all this delighteth the mind and bringeth health to the body" remarked Lawson in his 17th century opus *A New Orchard and Garden.*

As the informal landscape became popular, patios and gazebos stocked with chairs and umbrella tables were a part of the scene. The notion that turf seats belonged in the formal garden hastened their unpopularity. These manicured lawns are beautiful, but often too vast and remote to draw us into it. A garden should evoke intimacy, and turf seats can help restore that atmosphere.

Re-creating a turf seat is a joy. It is even more rewarding to occupy, and the only way to keep it healthy is to pamper it with a well placed posterior. Stone, brick, cement block, or wooden-tie containers can be constructed against a wall or fence, or used as free-standing planters on a patio.

A whiskey barrel cut in half is an excellent and inexpensive container for a turf seat. First, to extend its life, drill or saw drainage holes in the base. Second, raise it off the soil using flat stones or treated wood. The sitting height of the container should be about 18 to 22 inches. Third, fill it with a standard potting mix to which has been added a bucket of sand and a bucket of dolomite chips or oyster shell—a ratio of 10:1 soil to shell or chips. Water the adjusted mix and as it settles add more mix to keep the level of the soil flush with the top of the container.

One plant (four-inch pot size) will spread to cover one square foot the first season. Use from four to eight plants. Some herbs spread faster than others, but as a rule of thumb creeping thymes are fastest, then camomile. The slow-poke is Corsican mint. Be careful to look for bees before sitting.

These herbs grow best in full sun. Since frequent watering will lead to mineral depletion, add nutrients. As the herbs grow and spread, sit on them. Call it conditioning. This is the only gardening activity I know of that insists on inactivity for the health of our plants. It is important to press them into the soil regularly to encourage rooting all along their branches. Water to develop deep rooting. Rather than flooding the top, use a two-inch pipe embedded eight-to-ten inches in the center of the container to apply water. This method also keeps your clothing dry. At the base encourage more fragrant herbs to grow outward into the paving or onto a path or patio.

You may expand this treat for the feet into an herbal lawn. Use the same techniques as for quality grass lawns, substituting the turf-seat herbs and keeping them trimmed to one-half-to-one inch with a weedeater or mower. Herbal lawns, or meads, rarely need any care except for a top dressing of manure or mulch each fall. Fertilize twice yearly. If never mowing is more to your liking, a shady mead of sweet violets makes a pleasant yard, especially with bulbs planted everywhere. Many bulbs, like saffron, are delicately scented and if planted en masse are a treat for the nose. Sweet woodruff is another shady mead herb. You'll find yourself becoming lost in a patch as its flowers spread their scent into the cool, dark woodsy recesses of the garden. Flowering lasts for several weeks in the spring.

In a partially sunny spot mint, English pennyroyal, camomile and chives should accompany sweet woodruff and violets to contribute fragrance for the rest of the year. In late summer, before winter takes them all, harvest herbs for yourself, dry them and hang them swaglike on a door to freshen the air indoors, or crush them into a carpet before vacuuming for a fresh meadowlike scent.

Arranged in a patchwork quilt pattern,

herbs and alternating paving blocks can create an entertaining patio feature. Such checkerboard gardens were popular on country estates in the eighteenth-to-nineteenth centuries. Carpet-smooth and low-profile herbs were substituted for squares of paving in a ratio of 1:4 to 1:10. Taller herbs such as valerian, sweet fennel, and meadow sweet and fragrant shrubs and trees inhabited squares on the outer edges. All the year-round a table and chairs would be strategically relocated near the most alluring features.

Containers of fragrant herbs go well with this design. Even the oldest soliloquies speak of the merits of an urn overflowing with herbs. Urns, buckets and troughs offer a home for nature's finest aromatic annuals such as German camomile, coriander, sweet marjoram, and basil. The purple-hued 'Krishna', 'Dark Opal', and cinnamon basils are the most fragrant of this family. German camomile's spicy apple scent is welcome on any patio. Put them all together and add a pot of summer savory, and their combined scents are reminiscent of crowded spice markets.

Whether we enter or leave a garden we open a gate. It is the garden gate, with a garland of herbs that supplies the visitor with a summary of what is to come or what has been experienced. Yet opening a gate can be more than a mere action; the moment can become an event to remember. A gate door that clears the ground by six-to-eight inches as it swings will pass over herbs placed beneath it. The best herbs for this rough job are the mints: black, orange, ginger, spearmint, apple, lime, and pineapple. Prune them to force bushy growth and discourage flowering.

Equally as rewarding under the gate are lemon balm, camomile, costmary, santolina, clove pinks, and English pennyroyal. With every swing the gate creates its own perfume. It is a greeting and a farewell, an opening to a garden that is worth entering again and again.

Distinctive and Pleasing Fragrances From Trees, Shrubs and Vines

Gary L. Koller

In building a garden of fragrance one needs to look at trees to create the ceilings and upper walls of garden rooms, shrubs to form intermediate and low walls, as well as barriers, dividers and enclosures. Vines are efficient at conserving precious ground-level space while at the same time they can be used as upward-climbing green garlands that soften the harshness found in many urban landscapes. Woody plants are the elements that provide structure and form in the garden and landscape year-round. It is important to select them carefully so that they function as elements of structural design even when they are not emitting a scent or fragrance

Many plants are fragrant and this list only presents a handful of those available. In making selections my criteria included plants with fragrances strong enough to be detectable from a distance and fragrances that most people find desirable. (Many plants produce a fragrance that a majority of people find undesirable or offensive and these are not included.)

Before making a selection of any of these plants I recommend that you make a personal smell test to determine that the fragrance is one which pleases you.

Gary Koller is managing horticulturist at the Arnold Arboretum and a member of the Department of Landscape Architecture at Harvard University.

Fragrant Shrubs

Butterfly-bush (*Buddleia davidii*)
8-12 feet tall and 6-10 feet wide, full sun, hardy to 0 to −10°F.

A deciduous shrub that in the south can become large and open in habit while in northern areas is usually dense and bushy due to stem damage from winter cold. This plant blooms on new-season wood and even if it dies to the ground during winter, it will grow and bloom during the summer. Flowering occurs in midsummer and, depending on the cultivar, flowers range from white to pink, blue, and pale yellow. The blossoms are fragrant and they also provide visual enjoyment, as many forms of butterflies delight in this plant.

Carolina allspice (*Calycanthus floridus*)
6-9 feet tall by 6-10 feet wide, full sun to light shade, hardy to −20°F.

A large deciduous shrub that bears large leaves that are dark-green in summer and yellow and amber in the autumn. Flowers appear in midsummer. They are about two inches across and dark reddish-brown. The low visual profile is made up for by a strong, fruity fragrance. This plant is easily grown, and because of its healthy, dense foliage, it makes a desirable filler plant in a shrub border. One should note that in nurseries this species is often confused with another species that lacks floral fragrance. In order

Viburnum carlesii is a deciduous shrub that blooms in early May in the northeast. Buds are pale pink opening to white and intensely fragrant.

to make sure you are acquiring the most fragrant form, purchase this plant when in bloom and you can make a personal fragrance test.

Wintersweet (*Chimonanthus praecox*)
10-15 feet tall by 8-12 feet wide, full sun, hardy to 0°F.

A large deciduous shrub that bears deliciously fragrant flowers in early spring. A beautiful specimen was in bloom near the Haupt Conservatory of the New York Botanical Garden in February, 1989, following an unusually mild winter. Its early blossoms and intense fragrance attracted much attention. Because this plant is large and undistinguished after flowering it requires a location where it will be seen during the bloom period but where it can recede into the landscape at other times of the year. During severe winter conditions one should expect flower buds to blast or perhaps stems and twigs to die back.

Summersweet (*Clethra alnifolia*)
3-8 feet tall and 3-8 feet wide, full sun to light shade, hardy to −35°F.

In Massachusetts, late summer is the time when summersweet comes into its prime. It occurs as a native plant and inhabits low wet soils ranging in exposure from full sun to moderate shade. In the wild, this plant inhabits moist soils, but in the garden it is perfectly happy in drier acid soils. Flowers are borne in upright terminal panicles and are intensely fragrant. They are typically white, but pale pink selections are available from specialty nurseries. This plant is tolerant of salt spray from roads or maritime locations. It suckers up, forming dense colonies that make superb tall ground covers when massed together.

Sweetfern (*Comptonia peregrina*)
2-4 feet tall and 4-6 feet or more wide, full sun, hardy to −35°F.

This deciduous shrub forms a low mass that spreads slowly by underground stems. In New England, where it is native, it is one of the first plants to invade dry, sunny, inhospitable sites along highways. While it does not have spectacular flowers, fruit, or autumn color, it is distinguished all summer long for its dark, lustrous healthy-looking green foliage. It is the foliage that possesses the fragrance, for when brushed against or crushed it emits a pungent aroma. Because of its toughness and diminutive habit this native shrub deserves wider recognition as a garden plant.

Thorny elaeagnus (*Elaeagnus pungens*)
10-15 feet tall and 10-15 feet wide, full sun to light shade, hardy to 0°F.

A large, robust evergreen shrub valued for green foliage on the typical species, and visually striking variegated foliage on several cultivars. Blossoms appear in the autumn. They are small, tubular, and silvery-white in color. While they are often hidden or lost among the foliage, it is the fragrance of the flowers that attracts attention. The general habit of this plant is somewhat untidy, and as a result, pruning to modify shape may be desirable.

Fothergillas are deciduous shrubs that form multistemmed colonies. They bear unusual stubby bottlebrushlike flowers in early spring. Blossoms are creamy white, fragrant, and last approximately ten to fourteen days. Leaves resemble those on witch hazel plants but are smaller in size and scale. In summer they are medium green, but in autumn they become star performers, displaying foliage in saturated shades of yellow, orange, and bright red, depending on the degree of sunlight available.

Dwarf fothergilla (*Fothergilla gardenii*)
2-3 feet tall and 3-5 feet wide, full sun to light shade, hardy to −20°F.

Large fothergilla (*Fothergilla major*)
6-10 feet tall and 6-10 feet wide, full sun to light shade, hardy to −20°F.

Gardenia (*Gardenia jasminoides*)
4-6 feet tall and 4-6 feet wide, full sun to light shade, hardy to 20°F.

The gardenia we all know as a florist pot plant is hardy out-of-doors in southern states along the Gulf Coast. It is valued for its dense habit, rich glossy foliage, and ivory-white, fragrant blossoms that occur over an extended period of time. It is a bit fastidious about its environment, requiring a moist but well-drained acid soil with protection from winter winds.

Chinese witch hazel (*Hamamelis mollis*)
10-15 feet tall and 15-20 feet wide, full sun to light shade, hardy to 0 to −10°F.

A large deciduous shrub whose bold dark green summer foliage is followed by autumn colors of clear yellow to yellow-orange. Fragrant flowers, which appear in early spring, last for a period of two to three

weeks. Individual strap-shaped blossoms are small and bright golden-yellow. The plant is easily grown and dependable for an annual floral show. A cultivar that is just becoming available is 'Pallida', which has a soft yellow flower, rich fragrance, and a spreading crown. One of the hardiest cultivars is 'Brevipetala', a plant with a more upright habit that bears short golden-yellow blossoms.

English lavender (*Lavandula angustifolia*)
1-2 feet tall and 2-3 feet wide, full sun, hardy to −10°F.

An evergreen shrub that is commonly found in the herb garden where it can be grown as a spreading mound or tightly pruned to form a low hedge. The lavender-purple flowers that occur in midsummer are valued for use in sachets. Foliage is gray-green and fragrant.

Osmanthus (*Osmanthus* spp.)
8-25 feet tall, depending on species selected, full sun to moderate shade, hardiness varies from species to species with the most cold-tolerant surviving short periods below 0°F. One exception is *Osmanthus americanus*; a fine specimen of this grows out-of-doors at Spring Grove Cemetery in Cincinnati, Ohio.

Large broadleaved evergreens that bear small, creamy white, fragrant flowers largely hidden among the foliage. The fragrance of *Osmanthus fragrans*, the fragrant tea olive, is rich and powerful, with several blossoms providing enough fragrance to fill a small room. Most species become quite large and can be used in the landscape much as one would use a holly. One way to distinguish *Osmanthus* from holly (*Ilex*) is that the leaves of *Osmanthus* are opposite and those of *Ilex* are alternate. Like *Ilex*, *Osmanthus* is adaptable to pruning and shaping.

Mock orange (*Philadelphus* spp.)
Variable in habit according to cultivar but most are large and 10-12 feet tall with an equal spread, sun to moderate shade, many types are hardy to −20°F.

A deciduous shrub that I value for tolerance to shade, drought, and poor-quality, gravely soils. All forms have a single season of ornamental interest, which is at flowering. Blossoms are white, single to double, and selected cultivars have a rich scent. Fragrant selections include 'Avalanche', 'Conquete', 'Enchantment', 'Fleur de Neige', 'Innocence', 'Miniature Snowflake', 'Minnesota Snowflake', 'Perle Blanche', and 'Virginal', among others. My favorite cultivar is *Philadelphus coronarius* 'Aureus', which in Massachusetts produces a flush of chartreuse green foliage in May. This color fades to a more typical green after six weeks or so. The color transformation is refreshing, for it allows the scene in a garden to change over time. Other cultivars that I find useful for their fragrant flowers and compact habit are 'Avalanche', which attains a height of four feet and arches outward in fountainlike fashion, and 'Miniature Snowflake', which is full and dense and matures at three-to-three-and-a-half feet in height.

Japanese pittosporum (*Pittosporum tobira*)

10-12 feet tall and 10-20 feet wide, full sun to heavy shade, hardy to 30°F.

A dense, compact evergreen that bears small, fragrant, creamy-white flowers that fade to yellow with age. Tolerant of dry, hot locations, salt spray, and severe pruning. Tough and durable. Adapts to a cool greenhouse or atrium location.

Roseshell azalea (*Rhododendron prinophyllum*) (*R. roseum*)

2-10 feet tall with an equal spread, full sun to light shade, hardy to −35°F.

A deciduous azalea that bears bright pink, fragrant flowers in late spring. Summer foliage is bright green, followed by bronze in autumn. Extremely hardy and more tolerant of high pH soils than many ericaceous plants.

Swamp azalea (*Rhododendron viscosum*)

2-8 feet tall and 3-6 feet wide, full sun to light shade, hardy to −35°F.

A deciduous azalea of loose, open habit, spreading slowly by underground stems. Flowers occur in early summer and vary from clear white to pale pink. While this plant normally inhabits low wet soils it is tolerant of drier, more normal, garden conditions. Tough and long-lived, as exhibited by thriving century-old plants at the Arnold Arboretum.

Clove currant (*Ribes odoratum*)

5-7 feet tall and 5-8 feet wide, spreading by underground suckers, full sun, hardy to −20°F.

A medium-sized deciduous shrub of irregular habit and spread. Growth is strong and vigorous. Foliage is bluish-green in summer and reddish-bronze in the autumn. The flowers, which appear in midspring, are small, tubular, yellow, and strongly scented. It should be noted that this plant is an alternative host to a plant disease known as white pine blister rust, and in some locations growth of clove currant is restricted.

Rose (*Rosa* spp.)

Variable in height and spread depending on the selection, full sun, hardiness depends on cultivar selected.

Roses range from miniatures 12-15 inches tall to climbing types that in optimum conditions can grow 20-30 feet tall. They include species that occur in the wild through an innumerable list of cultivars. Some are intensely fragrant while many of the modern teas and floribundas have been developed for size and color rather than for intense fragrance. Why is it that one so often sees roses growing in shade, a habitat completely wrong for successful growth and exuberant flowering? Seek those types of roses that are fragrant, disease resistant, and hardy enough that they will not need winter protection in your area.

Japanese skimmia (*Skimmia japonica*)

3-4 feet tall with an equal spread, full sun to light shade, hardy to 0°F.

This evergreen forms a dense mound of light green foliage. Flowering occurs in midspring on separate male (staminate) and female (pistillate) plants. Flowers on male plants tend to be larger and have a stronger fragrance than those on female plants. In autumn female plants bear showy clusters of bright red, pea-sized fruit. A related species is *Skimmia reevesiana*, which is lower growing, more open in habit, and bisexual—meaning that with only one plant you can expect good fruit set.

Korean spice viburnum (*Viburnum carlesii*)
4-8 feet tall and 4-8 feet wide, full sun, hardy to − 20°F.

A deciduous shrub with a full, rounded habit. Flowers appear in early May in the Boston area. Individually small, they are borne in profusion in dense rounded cymes. Buds are pinkish red, opening to flowers of clear white that last 10-14 days. Fragrance is intense. Summer foliage is light green, and in autumn it turns to shades of red and purple. An alternate choice to this species is *Viburnum* x *juddii*, which is a hybrid with *Viburnum carlesii* as one of its parents. Many consider it a superior ornamental because of enhanced disease resistance and greater ease of propagation.

Fragrant Trees

Mimosa (*Albizia julibrissin*)
20-35 feet tall with an equal or greater spread, full sun, hardy to 0 to − 10°F.

The plant typically forms a low, broad, spreading canopy. Numerous small leaflets make up the tropical-looking, pinnately compound leaves. Blossoms, small and delicate brushlike clusters that vary in color from light to deep rose-pink, occur in midsummer, in great quantities. Flowers open over a period of several weeks, providing an extended bloom season.

Katsura tree (*Cercidiphyllum japonicum*)
40-80 feet tall with an equal spread, full sun to light shade, hardy to − 20°F.

The fragrance of this plant comes not from the flowers but from the senescent foliage in the autumn. Leaves are heart-shaped with scalloped edges, medium green in summer and golden to apricot during the autumn. Fragrance occurs as the leaves turn color and begin to fall away. The odor is sweet, pervades a large area surrounding the plant, and is quite ephemeral, lasting only a week or two.

Russian olive (*Elaeagnus angustifolia*)
12-20 feet tall with an equal spread, full sun, hardy to − 40°F

This tree is commonly grown in the upper midwest because of its tolerance to extremely cold temperatures, aerial salts, drought, alkaline soil conditions and wind. Foliage is distinctive for its silvery-gray appearance. Flowers occur in midspring and while small and relatively inconspicuous they do produce a delightful scent.

Clematis montana is a vigorous vine bearing glossy green and leathery leaves. Flowers are two or more inches across, white to pink depending upon the cultivar.

Southern magnolia (*Magnolia grandiflora*)

50-80 feet tall and 30-50 feet wide, full sun, hardy to 0°F.

A grand magnolia, of massive stature, native to the American South. The oval leaves are huge, dark green and glossy. The main flowering period is midspring but occasional flowers are borne all summer long. Blossoms are intensely fragrant, generally eight to twelve inches in diameter. Magnificent, historic specimens of this species flank the south entrance to the White House in Washington, D.C.

Bigleaf magnolia (*Magnolia macrophylla*)

30-40 feet tall and 20-30 feet wide, hardy to −10°F.

This magnolia bears the largest individual leaves of the genus, measuring one to three feet in length. Because of this size the leaves have a visually coarse texture. Blossoms occur in early summer and are distinctive for their large dimensions. Petals are thick in substance, dull creamy white, eight to fourteen inches across and highly fragrant.

Oyama magnolia (*Magnolia sieboldii*)

15-30 feet tall and 20-40 feet wide, full sun, hardy to −5°F.

In New England, June is the flowering period of this rare magnolia. It produces white cup-shaped blossoms with center tufts of scarlet stamens. Flowering continues for a period of several weeks. Best growth occurs in soils with an acid pH.

Star magnolia (*Magnolia tomentosa*) (*M. stellata*)

10-20 feet tall and 10-15 feet wide, full sun, hardy to −35°F.

One of the most common magnolias in the home landscape. Useful because of its smaller stature and ease of culture. Flowers occur in spring just before the leaves emerge, allowing all blossoms to be appreciated in one view. Colors are typically white but in the cultivar 'Rosea' there is a faint pink color. Because of the earliness of flowering, blossoms are sometimes damaged by frost. Be careful to select a site

Clematis paniculata *(sweet autumn clematis) is a deciduous vine that flowers in early autumn producing a multitude of small, white deliciously fragrant flowers.*

with an exposure that allows adequate air drainage so cold air will settle at a lower level than the one at which the plants grow.

Sweetbay magnolia (*Magnolia virginiana*)

20-60 feet tall with an equal spread, with the largest growth potential in southern climates, full sun, hardy to −10°F.

In northern areas this is a small tree, while in the southern part of its range it can become quite sizeable. There are two general forms—one that becomes deciduous in winter months and another known as *australis* that tends to be evergreen or semi-evergreen. The Arnold Arboretum recently introduced a cultivar known as 'Milton' that is fully evergreen in the Boston area. In New England, flowers occur in early June at a time when there is a full complement of foliage. Blossoms are two to three inches across, ivory white, and sweetly fragrant. Flowering occurs over a period of approximately three weeks. This tree grows equally well in wet to dry soils, but the growth habit changes depending on the environment. In dry soils the plant tends to have one or a few stems and in wet soils the plant becomes multistemmed.

Apple (*Malus* spp.)
20-50 feet tall with an equal spread, full sun, hardiness varies depending on the species or type selected.

Apples are common both as orchard trees and as ornamental flowering crab-apples. They are widely available, tough, hardy, and easily grown. Flowers occur in mid-May in New England, with all types compressed into a bloom period of about three weeks. Flower colors range from white through pink to reddish pink, and blossoms can be single to double, all depending on the type selected. Fruit can range from one-eighth-inch across to the size of the large apples found in supermarkets. Leaves are typically green, but some forms bear bronze to reddish-purple summer foliage. Many of the older types were highly susceptible to leaf and foliage diseases such as apple scab, cedar apple rust, and powdery mildew. Today, with the desire for low maintenance, it is important to select more disease-resistant forms for the landscape. Many apples tend to be alternate in their flowering and it might be wise to select varieties that are annual in flower and fruit production.

Royal paulownia (*(Paulownia tomentosa)*
40-45 feet tall with an equal spread, full sun, hardy to −10°F.

An example of an introduced tree that has made itself at home, this tree can be found naturalized through areas of the southeastern United States. It is valued for its rapid growth, clear white wood (prized by Asian people for furniture) and lavender blossoms that are an unusual color in north temperate trees. The Chinese plant paulownia because of its deep root system, which allows crops to grow directly up to the base of the tree.

Cherry (*Prunus* spp.)
10-35 feet with an equal spread, full sun, hardiness depends on the variety selected.

Cherries are well-known as garden plants and much loved for their early-season flowering—a symbol of the return of spring. Flowers vary in color from clear white to rich pink, depending on the type selected, and fragrance varies from species to species. Some types produce an edible fruit in early-to-midsummer. Species with fragrant flowers include *P. avium, P. caroliniana, P. cerasifera, P. mahaleb, P. mume, P. padus, P.* x *yedoensis*, among others.

Black locust (*Robinia pseudoacacia*)
30-50 feet tall and 20-35 feet wide, full sun, hardy to −35°F.

A native plant that is a pioneer, quickly invading disturbed soils and abandoned fields. While it can be grown with a single stem it suckers up and in the wild, tends to form thickets and colonies. *Robinia* is valued for its ability to inhabit dry, infertile soils. Foliage is dark green in summer and falls away in the autumn without any significant color change. The bark of this tree is blackish, deeply ridged, and visually distinctive. Pealike flowers, occurring in New England in early June, are borne in dense, white racemes four to eight inches long.

Sapphire berry (*Symplocos paniculata*)
10-20 feet tall with an equal spread, full sun, hardy to −20°F.

A small and tough tree. Blossoms occur in mid-May in the Boston area and last for seven to ten days. They are small and creamy white, with a delicate fragrance. In the autumn, fruit, the size of a small pea, turns bright turquoise blue and is quickly devoured by birds. Flowering and fruiting occurs in alternate years.

Japanese tree lilac (*Syringa reticulata*)
20-30 feet tall with an equal spread, full sun, hardy to −35°F.

A small tree that is well-adapted to urban and seacoast environmental conditions as well as to heat and drought. Flowering occurs in late spring in large pyramidal heads at the end of last season's growth. The flowers, which are creamy white, are individually quite small, but they are showy because of their abundance. Tree lilacs bloom at the same season as roses and can be combined with them to create floral pictures in the landscape. Olfactory perception of the fragrance of this plant varies; some find the odor pleasing, while others do not.

Linden (*Tilia* spp.)
40-80 feet tall and 30-50 feet wide, full sun to light shade, hardy to −20 to −35°F. depending on the type chosen.

Lindens are large forest trees that are often used as street or lawn trees. In youth they tend to form dense, upright ovals, but with age they spread out and open, forming statuesque specimens. As a group they flower in midsummer and bear small yellow-green blossoms heavy with a sweet scent. Lindens make excellent urban trees because of their resistance to environmental pollutants and to hot, dry conditions. One negative is that they are sometimes subject to sooty mold, which causes darkening of midsummer foliage.

Fragrant Vines

Armand clematis (*Clematis armandii*)
Height 5-20 feet or more, full sun, hardy to 20°F.

A vigorous-growing vine bearing beautiful foliage that is glossy green and leathery. Flowers occur in early spring and are two-to-two-and-a-half inches across, white to pale pink, depending on the cultivar selected, and richly fragrant. Flowering occurs on last year's growth.

Anemone clematis (*Clematis montana*)
Height 15-25 feet or more, full sun, hardy to −10°F.

A strong-growing clematis that flowers in midspring. Blossoms are two-and-a-half-to-three inches across, in shades of clear white to pale pink. Flowering occurs on old-season growth. In England this species of clematis is often planted to grow up and through a mature apple tree, clamber over an old evergreen such as a yew or an arborvitae, or thread its way through the canes of a climbing rose.

Sweet autumn clematis (*Clematis paniculata*)
Height 5-20 feet or more, full sun to light shade, hardy to −20°F.

A deciduous vine that flowers in early autumn producing a multitude of small, white, deliciously fragrant flowers. After flowering, seed clusters develop. Green at first, they turn pale beige-brown when ripe and bear delicate hairs that are extremely handsome when backlit by the sun. This plant flowers on new wood, which means that it can be cut to soil level each winter and still flower abundantly in the autumn. Beautiful when draped over a wall. Easier to cultivate than many of the larger-flowered types of clematis.

Common white jasmine (*Jasminum officinale*)
Climbing 15 to 40 feet, full sun, hardy to 10°F.

Deciduous or semievergreen vine. On the typical form flowers are white and appear from midsummer through early fall. In parts of southern Europe a variety, *affine*, whose flowers are tinged with pink and bear broader calyx lobes, is grown to be used in perfumery.

Japanese honeysuckle (*Lonicera japonica*)
Climbing 15 to 30 feet, full sun to moderate shade, hardy to −20°F.

A vine that is deciduous in the north and evergreen in southern areas. This is the honeysuckle vine that spreads like a weed through the woodlands of the mid-Atlantic states, carpeting the ground floor and clambering up the trees. In early summer it produces flowers that emerge white and fade to pale yellow. Blossoms are sweetly fragrant. While individual blooms are short-lived, flowering extends over a period of several weeks. I particularly like the vine for its late retention of foliage, which in Massachusetts turns a nice bronze color in late October and remains on the plant into the harshness of midwinter. This plant is excellent to weave through and mask a chain link fence. Cultivars which I like are 'Halliana', a good vigorous grower and 'Aureo-reticulata', with yellow netted markings through the leaves.

FRAGRANCE IN THE CITY GARDEN

Deborah Peterson

A garden in a city is a very special place: a quiet green oasis in a world of noise, concrete and steel. The owner of a city garden dreams of reading the Sunday papers while relaxing in this tranquil setting. He envisions himself listening to music on a moonlit night, or he makes plans for all the parties he wants to have in his Eden in the city. It is a refuge from the stresses of urban living, and it is richer if it is also a fragrant garden.

In contrast to this rather romantic view, the general public's concept of a urban garden is literally derived from the novel *A Tree Grows in Brooklyn*. To wit: any growth is a miracle. They expect long lists of pollution-sensitive plants and short lists of plants that thrive amid gas fumes and concrete.

The truth is almost everything grows in the city. This author can think of a short list of plants that may be pollution-sensitive—tuberous begonias, fuchsias, achimenes (all hanging basket subjects), some pines, and some over-

bred roses and rhododendrons. Plants cope with the bad air as well as people. Those that are frail will be affected and those that are hearty will not.

The City Garden

City gardens are gardens of extremes, from sunlit, windswept rooftops and penthouses to shady backyards of townhouses or cavelike balconies along the sides of highrises. There are fragrant gardens that will grow in all of these extreme situations. But each individual growing situation must be considered.

The growing conditions on a rooftop are most similar to those found at the seashore: high winds, brilliant light, and rapidly draining

Deborah Peterson, co-author of The Don't Throw It, Grow It Book of Houseplants *(Random House, 1977) and editor of* The Pits *(the newsletter of the Rare Pit and Plant Council), is a New York City landscape designer, garden writer and lecturer.*

Oxydendrum arboreum has fragrant panicles of white flowers in early summer that are exceptionally long lasting. Fall foliage color ranges from soft red through bright red to mahogany.

soil. These factors must be considered when selecting plants. There are many that will thrive under these conditions and others that only tolerate them. If, however, there is a plant that you simply must grow, try it by all means.

The rooftop gardener will have to grow plants in containers. There are many ready-made planters on the market. They must be constructed of an enduring material, such as wood or fiberglass. The best wooden containers are made of redwood, cedar, or treated pressed pine, and fastened together by screws. The planters should have feet so there is a space beneath for air circulation, and there must be drainage holes in the bottom. One of the best ready-made planters is a used whiskey keg cut in half or thirds. Two-thirds of a whiskey keg is ideal for a small tree. Trees and shrubs require a container that has at least a 24-inch diameter. Containers for flowering plants (annuals and perennials) should be at least 18-inches wide and 24-inches deep. Most hardware stores sell potting soil in 60 pound bags that they will deliver to the roof.

The backyard gardener will find conditions that are similar to those in the woods. His garden is shaded by other buildings and protected from wind. Light in the city garden is described as a "wandering ray"—brightly shining on the garden one moment only to retreat behind a building the next, and reappearing in another spot later in the day. Every garden, however, has at least one bright spot. The amount of light in the different areas of the garden will determine the placement of the plants.

Measuring the light is perhaps the most important step to be taken. Sun-loving plants, such as tea roses, require a minimum of six hours of sunlight a day. Plants that thrive in partial shade, such as rhododendrons, require at least four hours a day. Even plants that grow in dense shade, such as ferns, need filtered light. To measure your light, keep track of the light in the brightest part of the garden. How

long is the sun in that particular area? April/ May or September/October are the best months in which to measure the light; they are also the best months for planting. In June, July, and August, when the sun is directly overhead, the readings will be unrealistically high, and conversely, in November, December and February, they will be unrealistically low. The safest plants to choose for the backyard are those that require, or at least tolerate, partial shade.

Unlike the rooftop or terrace gardener, the backyard gardener does not have to import soil. The surface soil is frequently hardpacked and must be broken up with a rototiller or a pick-axe. Add peat and sand to enrich the soil. Our recipe for city soil is: ¼ builders sand, ¼ peat moss to ½ on-site soil. This may seem like hard work, but it is nothing compared to carting 15 cubic yards of loam from the sidewalk through the house to the backyard! The soil you build yourself will be better than any topsoil carted in from the suburbs.

City soil has an unexpected virtue. As you dig around your garden you will find a lot of rubble, from the surface down to two feet. Don't cart it off! All this debris will supply your plants with excellent drainage. To get rid of the surface rubble, dig a big hole, and as you work toss in any bricks and mortar that are lying on the surface. Cover the hole with soil and plant your most finicky plants on top. (Daphnes and rhododendrons love good drainage!)

The balcony gardener works between two extremes. He must grow all plants in containers like the rooftop gardener, but his garden will be almost as shady as that of the backyard gardener because his backyard has a roof.

The urban gardener has one advantage over his suburban counterpart. Cities are microclimates and are frequently ten degrees warmer than the surrounding towns. For example, in New York City the zone is 7 (0 to 10 degrees), and in nearby Westchester, the zone is 5 or 6 (0 to −10 degrees). This small difference in temperature allows the city gardener to grow many plants that could not survive the cold of our nearby suburbs.

If the city gardener takes these factors into consideration, he will find he can grow many plants in his fragrant garden.

Fragrance

Flowers are scented to attract pollinators. Plants that bloom in the early spring or the late fall are frequently heavily scented, as this is when pollinators are few and sluggish. White flowers tend to have more fragrance than brightly colored flowers. The latter attract their pollinators with their flashy colors.

Fragrance is a very elusive and individual quality. What is overpowering to one person will be delightful to another. Some people have a high degree of sensitivity to scent, while others have almost none. The sense of smell is one of the first senses to atrophy, and many older people have diminished ability to detect fragrance. Smoking can also reduce a person's ability to smell.

Plant breeders have done much to lessen the fragrance of plants. As species have been hybridized for bigger blooms, a wider range of color, or extended blooming season, their offspring have lost their parents' scent. Unfortunately scent is one of the first qualities to be lost in hybridization. Roses are an example. Most of the species roses are fragrant and very few of the hybrids are. When selecting the plants for your fragrant garden, take a sniff first.

The list that follows consists of plants that have proved their durability in the city. There are many more, so—experiment.

Fragrant Landscape Plants for the City[1]
Trees and Shrubs

	Zone	Height

Abelia grandiflora: glossy abelia

6-8　　5′

Abelias are delightfully fragrant evergreen shrubs that bloom from midsummer to hard

[1] FS = Full sun, PS = Partial shade; WR = Wind resistant, WP = Wind protection

frost. The flowers, borne in clusters, are bell-shaped, white with a blush of pink.

FS/PS　WP

Abeliophyllum distichum: white forsythia

4-9　　5′

White forsythia is a deciduous March-blooming shrub that takes some time to reach blooming size but is well worth the patience. The fragrant white flowers are borne on arching branches that cascade to the ground, making a glorious fountainlike display.

FS/PS　WR

Amelanchier: shadbush, serviceberry,

There are two amelanchiers that bloom in early June when the "shad" are running; hence the name. Both are fragrant and have blue berries that attract birds. The flowers are white and borne in small clusters. Colorful autumn foliage.　　FS/PS　WR

Amelanchier canadensis: shadblow

4-8　　60′

This is the largest of the common shadbushes. It is found growing wild throughout the Eastern U.S. The flowers are single, fragrant, and white, and they appear in June, just before the leaves break out. The autumn foliage is yellow to red, and the shrub has a very attractive grayish bark, which gives it winter interest.

FS/PS　WR

Amelanchier laevis: Allegheny shadbush

5　　35′

The Allegheny shadbush is a small, irregular-shaped tree that bears masses of fragrant white flowers in early spring.　FS/PS　WR

Chionanthus virginicus:

Virginia fringe tree　　3-9　　25′

Virginia fringe tree is an extremely delicate and graceful multistemmed tree that bears clouds of fragrant white flowers in June, followed by black fruit. It is quite late to leaf out in the spring and has colorful yellow foliage in the fall.　　FS/PS　WP

Cladrastis lutea: yellowwood　4-8　　9-30′

Yellowwood is a slow-growing tree that bears panicles of one-foot long pendulous flowers. It has lovely compound leaves that turn yellow in autumn.　　FS/PS　WR

Corylopsis pauciflora: 5-9   4-5′
Corylopsis is one of the earliest shrubs to bloom in the spring, bearing panicles of creamy-yellow bell-shaped flowers. A wonderful shrub for the shady yard.   PS   WP

Cytisus praecox: Warminster broom
                              5-8   6-8′
Warminster broom is an evergreen shrub with long pendulous branches that are covered with creamy-yellow pealike flowers in late spring. It needs full sun and excellent drainage. Broom is an ideal plant for the terrace.
                              FS   WR
Daphnes are among the most fragrant and loveliest of shrubs you can grow. They are a bit tricky, but if you can grow one daphne, you can grow all of them. They require excellent drainage and very good light. The author's greatest successes have been daphnes grown in rubble-filled city gardens.

Daphne x burkwoodii 'Somerset':
                              6-8   6′
This is a gracefully mounding evergreen shrub that is blanketed with fragrant pink flowers in May.   FS/PS   WP

D. x burkwoodii 'Carol Mackie':
                              4-8   6′
This daphne is very similar to the above, but has delicate white margins on the leaves.

D. cneorum: 4-8   9″-10″
Daphne cneorum is a delightful subshrub with needlelike foliage, a spreading habit and may be used in the front of the border or as a ground cover. These little plants are covered with clouds of small fragrant pink blooms in spring and again in the fall.   PS   WR

D. mezereum: February daphne
                              4-8   3′
This is the earliest of all the daphnes to bloom. It is a deciduous shrub that has rosy purple flowers that bloom on the old wood. The flowers are followed by bright red berries in June. There is a white variety, *D. mezereum* 'Alba'.

Franklinia: Franklin tree   5-9   25′
This is a choice deciduous tree that has fragrant white camellialike blooms beginning in August and continuing until frost. The leaves are an attractive bronze red, making a lovely contrast with the large white flowers. It is a native American tree that was found in Georgia in 1790 by John Bartram of Philadelphia. He brought the tree back to Pennsylvania and named it after his friend Ben Franklin. The tree has never been found growing in the wild again. It requires a moist growing situation.   PS   WP

Hamamelis: witch hazel. The earliest blooming shrubs, frequently blooming as early as February. All have fragrant flowers with ribbonlike petals that unfurl on a warm day and curl up with the cold. All can be grown in sun or partial shade. They are ideal for shady backyards.
Hamamelis x intermedia 'Arnold's Promise':
                              5-8   20′
'Arnold's Promise' has extra-large primrose-yellow flowers and brilliant orange fall foliage.

H. virginiana: common witch-hazel
                              5-8   15
This is a fall-blooming witch-hazel. It is the most shade-tolerant.

Illicicum floridanum: Florida anise bush
                              7-9   15′
The Florida anise bush is a curiosity for the urban garden. It is a native evergreen shrub with long dark aromatic foliage and star-shaped maroon flowers that are borne in mid-spring. The fragrance of the flowers appeals to some and repels others. However, this is a beautiful shrub and a conversation piece.
                              PS   WP
Ligustrum: privet
Perhaps the most overused and under-appreciated of shrubs in the landscape. Were an alien to drop down from outerspace in June, he would find the country blanketed in the heavy sweet aroma of privet and no doubt think the aroma wonderful. Mention privet to anyone else and they yawn.

These large shrubs or small trees are evergreen or nearly evergreen. They are extremely fragrant and will grow in full sun or dense shade, on the tops of mountains, or at the water's edge. They can be pruned to suit any landscape.

Ligustrum amurense: amur privet
4-9   10′
This is a fast-growing shrub with dark green leaves that has large racemes of very fragrant white flowers in June and July. The flowers are followed by attractive clusters of dark blue berries that attract birds.   FS/PS   WR

L. x ibolium: 4-9   8′
This privet is similar to the above but has dark, glossy green leaves.

L. ovalifolium: California privet.
7-9   15′
The California privet is evergreen and has glossier leaves. It is not as hardy as the others.
FS/PS   WR

Lindera benzoin: spice bush   5-8   12′
Spice bush is an excellent native shrub for a shady yard. The small yellow flowers are among the earliest to bloom in spring. The fragrance of the spice bush is in its leaves and twigs.   PS   WP

Lonicera fragrantissima: winter honeysuckle
6-9   FS/PS
Most of the honeysuckles are vines. This hardy semievergreen tree bears cascades of fragrant white flowers in midspring on old wood. The flowers are followed by attractive red berries.

Magnolias are a large family of trees and shrubs. Some are evergreen, and all bear gorgeous flowers, many of which are very fragrant.   FS/PS

Magnolia grandiflora: southern magnolia
7-9   40′
This is a very stately tree that has large glossy green leaves with a handsome brown indumentum on the undersides. The flowers, borne in late spring, are enormous white saucers that have a delicious fragrance. These trees are a bit large for the average city garden, and far too large for a container, but if you have space for a specimen tree, rank this high on your list.   FS/PS   WR

M. grandiflora 'Little Gem':   6-9   6-10′
'Little Gem' is a wonderful tough little tree that bears fragrant white flowers from April to July and again from September until the heaviest frost. It is slightly smaller than *M. grandiflora* but it has the same glossy foliage with brown undersides.   FS/PS   WR

M. loebneri: 4-9   25′
This is a lovely deciduous magnolia with fragrant star-shaped flowers that appear before the foliage in early spring.   FS/PS   WR

M. salicifolia: anise magnolia 6-9   30′
The slender aromatic leaves of this magnolia smell like anise when crushed. The flowers are white, fragrant, and borne in May.
FS   WR

Mahonia aquifolium: Oregon grape holly
5-9   3-6′
Oregon grape is a very handsome upright evergreen shrub with large dark green holly-like leaves. In April the plant bears dense clusters of fragrant sulphur-yellow flowers. These are followed by lovely light blue berries. The foliage takes on a beautiful bronze color in winter.   PS   WP

Mahonia bealei: leatherleaf mahonia
7-9   12′
The leaves of this mahonia are much larger, 12-16″, and darker than the above. It is a stunning foundation plant when mixed with other evergreens. The April-blooming flowers are more fragrant than those of *M. aquifolium*.
PS   WP

Malus (apple and crabapple family) All the crabapples have flowers with a slight fragrance. The ones listed below are the most fragrant and disease resistant.

M. baccata: Siberian crab   2-8   25′
The Siberian crab is a lovely vigorous tree that bears clusters of single white flowers in midspring. These are followed by small red fruits.
FS   WR

48

M. 'Edna Mullins': white weeping crab

5-8   15′

This is a graceful weeping tree whose boughs are covered with fragrant double-white blossoms in May. The fruits are a light salmon-coral color. It is an excellent container plant for the terrace.   FS/PS   WR

M. ioensis 'Plena': Bechtel's crab

2-8   25′

Bechtel's crab is a midspring blooming crab with fragrant double pink flowers that look like clusters of roses.   FS   WR

M. 'Red Jade':   4-8   15′

Red Jade is a superb weeping tree for containers. The branches cascade with fragrant white blossoms in spring and are covered with red fruits that last well into winter.

FS/PS   WR

Myrica pensylvanica: bayberry

6′   2-8

This shrub produces berries from which bayberry candles are made. The spring flowers are insignificant. The foliage and the lovely gray-blue berries are fragrant. They develop along the branches and twigs. Both male and female plants are necessary for the production of berries. Bayberries retain their leaves in their Southern range and during mild winters in the North.   FS   WR

Myrica cerifera: Southern wax myrtle

7-10   30′

Southern wax myrtle is an evergreen tree closely allied to Northern bayberry. The leaves and the fruits are smaller.

WR

Oxydendrum arboreum: sourwood

4-9   25′

Oxydendrum has small fragrant 8-10″ panicles of white flowers in early summer when few other trees are in bloom. The flowers are exceptionally long-lasting and remain on the tree into the fall. It has lovely red autumn foliage.   FS/PS   WP

Pieris japonica: Japanese andromeda

5-9   4-8′

This attractive broad-leaved evergreen makes wonderful foundation plants. *Pieris* is sometimes called the 'lily-of-the-valley' shrub because of its pendulous clusters of fragrant white bell-shaped flowers. There are many cultivars in the red tones.

PS   WP

Poncirus trifoliata: hardy orange

6-9   20′

This is a genuine citrus tree for Northern gardens. The small orange fruits are not edible, but the April-blooming flowers are just as fragrant as those of its Southern counterparts. The thorns are two inches long and quite vicious. It can be pruned to a low hedge. This is a very interesting and under-utilized plant.

FS   WP

Prunus: The cherries. Like the crabapples, most cherry flowers have some fragrance if you sniff long enough. The ones listed below have notable fragrance and are disease resistant.

Prunus avium 'Plena'   3-8   30-40′

This is one of the hardiest cherries available. In mid-spring it is covered with fragrant double white flowers. It has handsome yellow autumn foliage.   FS   WR

P. x cistena: purple-leaved sand cherry

3-8   8′

The sand cherry has unique purple foliage that makes this an outstanding specimen whether it is in bloom or not. The flowers, white flushed with pink, bloom in late spring.

FS   WR

P. laurocerasus: cherry laurel 6-9   3-4′

This is a wonderful evergreen shrub that produces racemes of creamy white flowers in the late spring. Flowers are followed by tiny black cherries. This European cherry has been popular since Colonial times.   PS/PS   WP

P. padus: European bird cherry

3-8   45′

Lovely fragrant white racemes cover this tree in early May.   FS   WR

P. subhirtella 'Autumnalis': autumn flowering cherry   5-8   15′

Do not be misled by the name; this tree has only a few flowers in autumn; the main flush of bloom is in midspring. It is a particularly lovely tree with long pendulous branches covered with almond-scented white-pink flowers. It makes a stunning terrace specimen.

FS/PS   WR

Raphiolepis indica: Indian hawthorn

8-10   5'

Indian hawthorn is a delightful spring-blooming evergreen shrub for warm climates or very protected sites in the North. The pink flowers are borne in small panicles.   FS/PS   WR

Raphiolepis umbellata: Yeddo-hawthorn

7-9   6'

The Yeddo-hawthorn is a hardier variety of the above, but the flowers are white.

Rhododendrons and azaleas: All azaleas are rhododendrons. That is the only secure statement that can be made about this very large group of deciduous and broad-leaved evergreen shrubs. A weak rule of thumb: "The small-leaved deciduous rhododendrons are called azaleas". As with all such rules, there are many exceptions.

Of the typical broad-leaved (large leaved) evergreen rhododendrons there are species that are faintly fragrant:

Rhododendron fortunei: 6-9   5'

The rosy-lilac flowers are borne in late May and are moderately fragrant.   PS   WP

R. scintillans: 5-8   5'

Lovely clear pink tresses adorn this shrub in late May.   PS   WP

The following are deciduous small-leaved rhododendrons usually referred to as azaleas. Many are very fragrant, and most have lovely orange-yellow-red autumn foliage. All can grow in full sun or partial shade and all are wind resistant.

R. arborescens: sweet azalea   5-8   8-20'

Lovely white flowers fill the air with a heliotrope scent in June and July.

R. austrinum: Florida flame azalea

7-9   8-10'

An American native that bears exceptionally fragrant orange-yellow flowers in May.

R. schlippenbachii: royal azalea

5-8   5'

This azalea has very unusual foliage, almost round with a roughened texture. The foliage turns a lovely red in autumn. The flowers, which bloom in May, are soft pink and slightly fragrant.

R. viscosum: Swamp azalea   4-8   8

This lovely fragrant native bears small white flowers in June and July.   FS/PS   WR

Rhus aromatica: Fragrant sumac   3-8   3'

The graceful yellow flowers of this small tree have no fragrance, but the foliage is very aromatic. The flowers are followed by large conical red fruits that stay on the shrub all winter. Sumacs have brilliant autumn foliage.

FS   WR

Sarcococca hookeriana var. *humilis*: sweet box   6-9   1'

Sweet box is a charming glossy-leaved evergreen subshrub that has fragrant white flowers in spring, followed by long-lasting blue fruits. If tacked down it can be trained as a ground cover.   PS   WP

Styrax obassia: fragrant snowball

6-9   30'

S. obassia is the only fragrant member of this genus. The white flowers are borne in terminal racemes six-to-eight-inches long in June. This is a slow-growing tree that can tolerate a moderate amount of shade.   FS/PS   WP

Syringa: lilacs. Not all lilacs are fragrant, check before you purchase. They bloom at the height of spring in mid-May. They are, however, prone to mildew (a powdery fungus that forms on the leaves in mid-summer). The mildew doesn't seem to hurt the trees, but it doesn't enhance their appearance.

Syringa patula 'Miss Kim':   4-8   5'

'Miss Kim' is an ideal lilac for the smaller city garden. The pink flowers that bloom two weeks after the standard lilacs change from light pink to ice blue as they mature.

FS/PS   WR

S. persica: Persian lilac   5-8   8'
The graceful arching branches of Persian lilac make it an attractive plant year-round. It is stunning when it is covered with panicles of pale lavender flowers.   FS   WR

S. vulgaris: common lilac   4-8   15'
This is our lovely native lilac of "by the dooryard blooms" fame. In May it has lavender flowers that are deliciously fragrant.

Viburnums are truly shrubs for all seasons. In the spring they are covered with masses of white flowers, many of which are fragrant. In the summer their crisp green foliage adds a touch of coolness to the garden and in autumn, becomes a blaze of color. Many develop attractive red or black berries that remain on the shrubs through the bitterest months of winter.

V. x carlcephalum: fragrant snowball
                    5-9   8'
The snowball viburnum blooms in May with rounded clusters of white flowers. It has excellent autumn foliage, but no berries.
                    FS/PS   WR

V. x bodnantense: Bodnant viburnum
                    6-8   10'
The sweet-scented flowers have rich red buds that open to white with a pink flush. Bodant viburnum is the earliest blooming of the viburnums; the flowers may open as early as February in a mild winter. It has lovely autumn foliage.

V. x juddii: 4-8   7'
This is a very ornamental viburnum with waxy fragrant flowers that are borne in May and followed by black fruits. It has a spreading habit of growth.

V. x burkwoodii: 6-8   10'
In the South this viburnum is evergreen. It flowers in April with lovely pink buds opening to white flowers that are very fragrant. The autumn foliage is purple and the fruits are red-purple.   FS/PS   WR

Vitex agnus-castus 'Latifolia': chaste tree
                    8-15   7-10'

Vitex is a gorgeous small tree whose flowers, foliage and wood are fragrant. The tall blue racemes appear in late summer when little else is in flower. The foliage is silver-gray and palmate. It is lovely when underplanted with late-blooming pale yellow daylilies.
                    FSW   R

Fragrant Ground Covers

	Zone	Height	Light

Arctostaphylos uva-ursi: bearberry
                    3-8   4-6"
A charming native evergreen ground cover with small shiny leaves. It is covered with small pink flowers in mid-spring.
                    F S

Convallaria majalis: lily-of-the-valley
                    3-9   8"
A deciduous ground cover whose very fragrant bell-like blossoms are used in perfume. These carefree little plants bloom in June.
                    S

Dianthus: border pinks   3-8   6-12"
These little plants form tufted mounds of silvery, evergreen foliage. The small carnationlike flowers bloom from late spring until early fall. Not all members of this family are scented. The following have fragrance: *D.* 'Aqua,' single white; *D.* 'Essex Witch,' double pink; 'Her Majesty,' double white; & 'Old Spice,' double salmon.

Galium odoratum: sweet woodruff
                    4-8   8"
Both the leaves and the flowers of this deciduous plant are fragrant. The flowers, which bloom in May and June, are white. These are lovely soft plants that will grow almost anywhere. They spread rapidly but are not invasive.
                    PS

Hosta: 3-10   18"
These large plants fill in along shady paths or under trees. Only two of the species are truly fragrant: *Hosta plantaginea* and one of its hybrids, *H.* 'Royal Standard'. Both bear bell-

shaped white flowers that are held high above the foliage on three-foot stems.

S

Pachysandra terminalis: Japanese spurge
4-8   8"

The very toughest of all fragrant ground covers, it will grow anywhere, spreads rapidly, and blooms profusely in spring with small white fragrant flowers.

S

Phlox subulata: moss pinks
2-9   6"

These are wonderful little evergreen plants for the front of the border. The foliage is needlelike and forms tidy spreading mounds. In the spring they are covered with small fragrant star-shaped flowers. They are available in red, pink, white and blue.

FS

Thymus serpyllum: mother of thyme
3-9   2"

Perhaps the most elegant of all the fragrant ground covers. The evergreen foliage hugs the ground and is sturdy enough for limited foot traffic. It looks wonderful between stepping stones. In late May the little plants begin to bloom with tiny fragrant flowers that last until fall.

FS

Fragrant Roses for the City

There are three classes of roses that do very well in the City. *Rosa rugosa* roses and their hybrids can take the intense light, high winds, and semiarid conditions of the rooftop. Musk roses and their hybrids do well in the filtered light of the shady garden. Shrub and grandiflora roses need a bit more light than the musk roses, but can flourish in the sunniest section of a garden or do very well in the rugged conditions of the rooftop. Tea, Damask, and Bourbon roses tend to be a bit frail for city conditions. The list that follows is based on personal experience; there are many more roses that could be added to it.

	Color	Height	Type

Shrub Roses:

| 'Angel Face' | Lavender | 5' | Floribunda |

One of the few true lavender flowers in the rose family. They are double, extremely fragrant, and repeat throughout the season.

| 'Harrison's Yellow': | Yellow | 10' | Musk PS |

Double yellow flowers with a wonderful spicy fragrance cover this gorgeous rose in early May. One-time bloomer.

| 'Iceberg': | White | 4' | Shrub S |

An everblooming shrub rose with a heavenly fragrance. The author has picked buds from this rose in January.

| 'Betty Prior' | Pink | 4' | Shrub PS |

Lovely, slightly fragrant single pink flowers that are borne from May to frost. A very durable rose for the city.

Ramblers, climbers & pillar Roses:

| 'Don Juan' | Red | 12' | Climber PS |

Stunning dark-velvety double-red fragrant flowers make this an eye-catching rose. Repeat bloomer.

| 'Kathleen': | White | 7-15' | Musk PS |

Single blue-white flowers and pink buds seem to sparkle all season long on this dainty climber.

| 'Pink Pillar': | Pink | 8' | Brownell S |

Lovely double pink blooms with a very distinctive citrus fragrance are borne all season long on this sturdy rambler.

Rugosa roses:

| 'Agnes' | Yellow | 6' | Shrub FS |

The only yellow rose in the rugosa family. Small double yellow fragrant flowers cover the plant in June; a smattering of blooms during the rest of the season. Somewhat tangy fragrance.

| 'Alba': | White | 4' | Shrub FS |

Lovely single white flowers develop simultaneously with large red hips all season long. The hips remain on the plant well into winter.

'Frau Dagmar Hartopp':

| | Pink | 3' | Shrub PS |

A very heavy name for a delightfully fragrant dainty pink rose. The pink flowers are borne simultaneously with the longlasting red hips throughout the season.

'Hansa': Red/Purple 5'   Shrub FS

The double red-purple flowers have the distinct fragrance of cloves. A repeat bloomer that develops dark red hips.

Miniature Roses

Tough is the last word you would ever use to describe these delicate little plants, but tough they are! They can be grown in all parts of the country, and they withstand tremendous heat and cold. They do not require as much sun as standard roses, which makes them excellent candidates for backyard and balcony gardens, and they can take all the wind and intense sun of the penthouse and rooftop garden. They are all nonstop bloomers from May to December. There are hundreds of these little roses on the market now. Those listed below are the most fragrant ones in the author's collection.

R. 'Jean Kenneally' is larger than the other miniature roses and forms a dense little shrub 30″ by 30″. The flowers are a lovely shade of apricot.
R. 'Jennifer' is double light pink shrub-type rose. 15-18″
R. 'Julie Ann' is a hybrid tea with double vermilion flowers. 12-14″
R. 'Summer Butter' has pale yellow flat double flowers. 14-18″
R. 'Sachet' is a double damask-type rose with pale lilac blooms. 24″

Fragrant Vines

	Zone	Height

Actinidia species: These species offer lovely fragrant flowers and delicious fruit. All are very vigorous and require sturdy trellises. Male and female plants are required for fruit.

| *A. arguta:* | 4-8 | 100' |

The leaves are soft green with red petioles. The fruits are one inch in diameter and very sweet. It is said one vine can yield 100 pounds of fruit a year.

| | S-PS | WR |

| *A. chinensis:* | 7-8 | 100' |

This is the kiwi of commerce whose oval fuzzy fruit is sold year-round in grocery stores. The leaves are heart-shaped and slightly fuzzy. They are hardy to New York City.

| | S-PS | WP |

| *A. kolomikta:* | 3-8 | 100' |

The leaves of this kiwi are tri-colored—pink, green, and white. It is extremely hardy. The fruits are similar to those of *A. arguta.*

| | S-PS | WP |

| *Clematis maximowicziana:* | 3-9 | 30' |

The fragrance of sweet autumn clematis can perfume the whole neighborhood in the month of August. The flowers are small and star shaped and are followed by fluffy seed heads.

| | S-PS | WP |

| *Gelsemium sempervirens:* | 7-9 | 20' |

Double Carolina jessamine is a vigorous evergreen vine which is covered with one-inch fragrant yellow flowers in spring and summer.

| | S-PS | WR |

| *Hydrangea anomala petiolaris:* | | |
| | 5-9 | 60' |

The climbing hydrangea is one of the most elegant vines you can grow. The fragrant white flowers are borne in flat clusters that are six inches long. It climbs on arbors and walls without support. However, its clinging tentacles can damage wood. Rather slow to get started but well worth the wait.

| | S-PS | WR |
| | S-PS | WP |

Lonicera: honeysuckle
There are many species of these very fragrant, albeit aggressive vines. All are hardy from zones 5-9, can attain a height of 10-15' and will

perform best in full sun, but can take some shade. All are wind resistant.

L. heckrottii: (golden flame honeysuckle), pink outside, creamy yellow inside.

L. japonica 'Halliana': (Hall's honeysuckle) Creamy flowers all summer.

L. henryi: The long dark green foliage persists all winter even in the coldest areas. The lovely creamy flowers are followed by black fruit.

Wisteria species: These are lovely fragrant vines that are closely associated with the older sections of cities. The long ropy trunks scramble up sides of brownstones and cascade over iron fences. Their fragrance is delicate and the long pendulous racemes of blue or white flowers look lovely against bricks and brownstones.

These are very vigorous vines and all have the potential to reach well over 100 feet. All require a sunny position for maximum bloom. They can be grown in zones 4-9.

Unfortunately, they can be quite destructive. They can very easily take down telephone wires and become entangled in other structures. Very old vines have quite a bit of dead wood and can become fire hazards should a spark from a chimney land in them.

W. sinensis: (Chinese wisteria) Lovely fragrant pendulous blue flowers in May and again in August.

W. floribunda: (Japanese wisteria) The lovely pendulous lilac flower-clusters have been measured at two-and-one-half feet long.

W. floribunda 'Ivory Tower': A cultivar of *W. floribunda* that has pure white flowers and was discovered on the Princeton campus. ❧

Oxydendrum arboreum, *sorrel tree, has small fragrant panicles of white flowers that remain on the tree into fall complementing the lovely red foliage that ranges from soft red through bright red to mahogany.*

The Fragrant Old Roses

Page Dickey

For a glorious month, from late May to the end of June, my garden (55 miles north of New York City) is heady with the fragrance and lavish bloom of the old shrub roses. These roses are planted in a variety of garden beds where they combine charmingly with perennials, herbs, bulbs and ground covers. When not in bloom, they add structure to the gardens without casting too much shade, allowing flowers to weave through and beneath their branches.

Photos by Page Dickey

". . . in the hardy borders, among the Irises, Sweet Williams, Peonies, Sweet-scented Valerian and Canterbury Bells, [the old-fashioned Rose] has a very distinct place and lends to any garden an abiding charm and sweetness that cannot but be a delight to its possessor."
Louise Beebe Wilder
Adventures in a Suburban Garden, 1931

Top: Apothecary's rose, Rosa gallica officinalis, *was esteemed for its scent and its medicinal properties in the Middle Ages. The flowers are brilliant light crimson, semidouble with yellow stamens.*

'Blanc Double de Coubert' is a rugosa rose that blooms in May. The flowers are loosely double and are complemented by the handsome, glossy, deep green foliage.

Page Dickey gardens in northern Westchester County, New York, where she lives with family and assorted farm animals. She is currently writing a book about her life there.

The display starts quietly in the middle of May with the lovely old-fashioned yellow roses. The fern-leaved 'Father Hugo' (*Rosa hugonis*) opens sprays of butter-yellow single flowers on delicate arching twigs. Its sport, *Rosa cantabrigiensis,* is a treasure in my garden. (I have only seen it one other place — at Sissinghurst some years ago.) Its flowers are a paler yellow, luminous really, on a slender shrub that is sweetly scented. The hybrid rugosa 'Agnes' blooms now, soft yellow double flowers that are deliciously fragrant. It makes a tall shrub eventually and has dark green crinkly rugosa foliage.

By the end of May, two other rugosa roses are in full bloom in my garden and fill the air with their fragrance. Bushes of 'Blanc Double de Coubert' (four to five feet high) are planted in the corners of my small patterned white garden. Their papery chalk-white flowers (loosely double) are handsome against glossy deep-green ribbed leaves. After the first great flush of bloom, one can expect an occasional flower through September. The rugged foliage stays good-looking all summer and in October turns a pleasing yellow. In the herb garden surrounded by lamb's-ears and lady's mantle, 'Frau Dagmar Hartopp' opens large simple flowers of silvery-pink, with a center of yellow stamens. By late summer, if I haven't dead-headed the faded flowers, this small (three feet) bush is covered with wonderful hips, the size and color of cherry tomatoes. The rugosas seem to be disease-free; even the persistent Japanese beetles find their glossy leaves unpalatable.

I love to bury my nose in the first early blooms of the hybrid burnet rose, 'Stanwell Perpetual'. It is a four foot arching shrub, very prickly, with small ferny leaves and ruffled blush-pink flowers of intense old rose sweetness. Gertrude Jekyll (in *Roses for English Gardens*) recommends planting it in clumps of three, but my one bush looks graceful enough against a low stone wall where it is underplanted with mounds of pale pink *Geranium sanguineum* var. *prostratum.* It is a fountain of bloom in early June and continues to flower lightly until frost.

By the second week in June, the garden is a riot of rose bloom, and much time is spent wandering around the borders drinking in this extravagance of flower and fragrance. Damasks and albas, gallicas and centifolias, portlands and moss roses tumble about stands of foxgloves and campanulas, bushes of southernwood and rue, carpets of *Nepeta,* lamb's-ears and pinks.

I think the albas are my favorites. They make lovely graceful bushes (five or six feet in height, four or five feet wide) with arching branches of fresh blue-green foliage. Like most of the old roses, they have only one stretch of flowering, but with good shape and leaves, they stay a pleasing background all summer. And their blossoms! Pink to white, ruffled and swirled, sweetly, delightfully fragrant. 'Céleste' (or 'Celestial') is at the top of the list with enchanting flowers of pale pink somewhere between single and double. Here, bushes of 'Céleste' thrive in a half-shaded border with white and blue peachbells (*Campanula persicifolia),* yellow daylilies and soft-pink *Geranium macrorrhizum.* 'Maiden's Blush' is another five foot beauty, with blush-pink double flowers, a favorite cottage flower for centuries. In his classic book on old roses, Graham Stuart Thomas says "to me there is no rose scent so pure and refreshingly delicious as that of the 'Maiden's Blush'." 'Queen of Denmark' ('Konigin von Danemark') is similar but with deeper pink flowers that remind me of swirled strawberry ice cream. It jostles for space in my garden between the dwarf Korean lilac and bushes of *Baptisia,* and is underplanted with clumps of rue and coralbells. 'Félicité Parmentier' is a narrower shrub with smaller swirled blooms of the palest pink, fading to white. It mixes prettily with spotted foxgloves and the milky-blue bells of *Campanula lactiflora* in one of my sunny borders.

The large globular blooms of the centifolia, or 'Cabbage' rose, are familiar to us in Dutch and French floral art of past centuries. A common cottage plant in Gertrude Jekyll's day, she wrote "no rose surpasses it in excellence of scent; it stands alone as the sweetest of all its kind, as the type of the true rose smell." 'Fantin Latour' is a tall arching centifolia, remarkably thornless, that becomes a fountain of romantic blooms. The drooping flowers are large and packed with petals, a medium-to-pale pink, richly fragrant. Measuring five feet by five feet, it is a good rose for the corner of a garden bed. Next to 'Fantin Latour' in my flower border and often intertwined with it is the 'Common Moss' (*R. centifolia* 'Muscosa') a sport of the centifolia, beloved by the Victorians. It is a tall gaunt shrub with blooms that are similar to 'Fantin Latour' in fragrance and shape, but has fuzzy or mossy sepals that enfold its buds and frame its flowers. A posy of moss roses with some sprigs of southernwood and apple mint is a memorable treat. Three other centifolias grow in my garden. 'Petite de Hollande' is a small shrub (three feet) with charming miniature cabbage blooms that are clear pink and sweetly fragrant. 'Rose de Meaux', equally small and scented, has tiny pink pompom blooms. Dean Hole, the Victorian rosarian, calls them "the pony roses" of his childhood. The lovely buds are valued for potpourri. The third rose, 'Striped Moss', is a rather wayward shrub with small appealing flowers that are striped crimson and pale pink, framed with the telltale mossy sepals.

The ancient damask roses, softly colored and intensely fragrant, have always been cherished as a source for attar of roses, rose water and potpourri. Perhaps the most famous damask today is the beautiful 'Madame Hardy'. It is a stout five-foot bush literally covered with small white double blooms that open flat, swirled and quartered around a curious green button eye. The flowers are unique and sumptuous. The foliage is bright green, alas, appealing to Japanese beetles, and often looks ratty later in the season. I mask this with Michaelmas daisies, summer phlox and the late-blooming *Hosta* 'Honeybells'. Earlier, magenta-pink *Geranium sanguineum* and cheerful yellow evening primroses complement the white roses. 'Celsiana' is a favorite damask in my herb garden—very feminine ruffled pink blooms on a slight arching four-

foot shrub with downy light-green leaves. It has an exquisite fragrance. The venerable 'Autumn Damask' ('Quatre Saisons', *R. damascena bifera*), which repeats its flowering into October, is one of the most fragrant of all. Although the bush is somewhat scraggly, I prize the sweet loosely double flowers of clear pink and collect them carefully in baskets to dry for potpourri.

Similar in shape and scent to the damasks, the 19th century portland roses delight us with a second flush of flowering in late summer that is equal to, if not lovelier than, their first. Not growing as tall or as wide as most of the old shrub roses, they are ideal for the small garden. 'Comte de Chambord' makes a neat four foot by three foot shrub at the entrance to my garden. It has rich pink double flowers, deeply scented, that are born singly and are closely framed with large green leaves. Graham Stuart Thomas describes this portland characteristic as the "high shouldered" look. Smaller in stature with flowers a lighter pink, 'Jacques Cartier' is another portland treasure with a heady fragrance. Two bushes of this sweet rose stand across from 'Comte de Chambord', underplanted with lady's mantle and interwoven with regal lilies.

The gallica roses are the oldest of all the shrub roses and encompass some of the liveliest colors in their flowers. They tend to be compact bushes, almost thornless, with dark green leaves flowering only once in June for two or three weeks. The flowers have a light delicious fragrance that intensifies when dried and, consequently, the petals are prized for potpourri. The 'Apothecary's Rose' (*R. gallica officinalis*) was esteemed not only for its scent but for medicinal properties in the Middle Ages. On a low (three foot) spreading bush, masses of large, brilliant light crimson flowers, semidouble with yellow stamens, make a gorgeous display. Its sport, 'Rosa Mundi' (*R. gallica versicolor*) is the best of the striped roses. The same large semidouble petals are splashed and ribboned with white and deep pink. Both these striking roses grow in my herb garden, where they are surrounded by the soft foliage of wormwood, lamb's-ears and southernwood, bordered with thyme and spicy pinks. 'Tuscany Superb' is a stunning gallica with semidouble flowers of the deepest velvet crimson, showing golden stamens. It makes a fine picture underplanted with white and green variegated hosta (*H.* 'Thomas Hogg') and pale pink astilbes. The gallica 'Charles de Mills', with wonderfully swirled flowers of rich crimson-purple, is a conversation piece in my garden, tangling with the blush-pink climber 'New Dawn' and fronds of dark green tansy. 'Belle de Crécy' is a slight shrub with curious gallica blooms of blue-pink fading to mauve and gray. It grows here in a tangle with 'Madame Hardy' and another striped gallica 'Camaieux' which has stunning small double flowers. They open blush-white striped with light crimson, change to purple-crimson and fade to pale lilac and white.

The great Victorian shrub roses, the bourbons and hybrid perpetuals, are not always reliably hardy for me (Zone 5), but it is well worth taking the chance and growing a few of them. 'La Reine Victoria' and its sport 'Madame Pierre Oger' are tall narrow shrubs with charming cupped blooms, very round and double, the former a rich silky pink, its offspring pale, pale pink tinged with rose. Both are elegant flowers, sweetly scented, offered throughout the season. A favorite hybrid perpetual that is hardy in my garden is 'Baronne Prévost'. It is a good-sized shrub (four to five feet) with large handsome flowers of deep rose-pink, very double, opening flat and quartered with a button eye. It is richly scented. 'Reine des Violettes' is usually listed as a hybrid perpetual, but in habit and flower resembles the older shrub roses. It makes a large arching bush in my garden with almost thornless canes well-furnished with gray-green leaves. There is nothing quite like the color of its fragrant flowers. From a red-purple bud, the flower expands flat and swirled to a beautiful soft violet. Blooming quietly through the summer, 'Reine des Violettes' makes a lovely picture grown with pale yellow daylilies, white summer phlox and bil-lows of *Artemisia* 'Silver King'. Peter Beales says in his *Classic Roses,* "If I had to choose just one hybrid perpetual, it would have to be this one."

There are many excellent modern shrub roses popular now — 'The Fairy', 'Seafoam' and 'Bonica' come to mind — that offer a profusion of bloom throughout the summer and have some of the grace of the old roses. But they are missing what is, for me, a key ingredient — that intoxicating, deeply satisfying old rose scent. To thrill the nose as well as the eye, return to the romantic old shrub roses. ❧

Some Sources for Old Shrub Roses

Roses of Yesterday and Today
Browns Valley Road, Watsonville, California 95076-0398
Pickering Nurseries Inc.
670 Kingston Road, Pickering, Ontario LIV 1A6
Wayside Gardens
1 Garden Lane, Hodges, South Carolina 29695-0001
White Flower Farm
Litchfield, Connecticut 06759-0050
Claire's Nursery (not mail-order)
Haviland Hollow Road, Patterson, New York 12563
A source for all old roses in commerce can be found in the *Combined Rose List,* 1989, combined by and available from Beverly R. Dobson, 215 Harriman Road, Irvington, New York 10533 $11.50.
Bev Dobson's Rose Letter, published every other month. Same address. Subscriptions, $9.00 a year.

Fragrant Trees, Shrubs and Vines

Jerry Sedenko

The larger features of a landscape, the trees, shrubs and vines, are used for their architectural value. They give mass, substance and line to a garden. Aside from their forms and leaf and branch texture, fall foliage and flowers are also considerations for choosing such plants. But why choose a plant on a purely visual basis? One that gives fragrance adds a whole new dimension of enjoyment to the garden.

There are basically two sources of fragrance in any plant, blossoms being the most obvious. But leaves can also offer pleasant aromas, usually of a more resinous nature. Many foliage fragrances are only released when the leaves are bruised or brushed against. These are most effective near pathways and other areas of coming and going.

Wisterias are generous with their fragrance when in bloom. This one blooms in May in the northwest.

Even with flowers, scent is not always "free on the air." Most roses need to have a nose inserted before the fragrance is apparent. Yet no one objects. That's part of the experience of a rose. Other plants perfume the air around them for yards, and it is best to consider prevailing wind direction when siting these, so as to take full advantage of the situation. Some are fragrant only on warm days, some perfume the night air, and others release their aromas after a rain. With the lack of insect pollinators in the cold winter and early spring months, many plants that bloom at that season try to make themselves particularly attractive by being very powerfully fragrant.

Jerry Sedenko is a horticulturist and garden designer who lives and gardens in Seattle. He is an active member of the Northwest Perennial Alliance and the Hardy Plant Society. His articles appear in many gardening magazines.

Photos by Jerry Sedenko

The sense of smell is extremely subjective. Some fragrances can be delightful to some, but annoying to others. A cloying sweetness, a piercing sharpness, or a fetid aroma are all generally considered to be unpleasant, so the list I have prepared attempts to steer clear of such fragrances. However, bear in mind that some fragrances, like night-blooming jasmine, can be delightful at ten paces, but are nauseatingly sweet at two feet.

My list is also confined to plants that are generally available to a gardener without too much trouble. Therefore, sources for many of these things are listed at the end.

Trees With Fragrant Flowers

Acacia baileyana, dealbata, smalli, often called mimosa, particularly in the florist trade. These, the hardiest members of the Australian section of this genus, are widely planted where adapted. In February, the feathery gray leaves are bespangled with clusters of half-inch primrose pompoms, with a cinnamon scent that carries well on the breeze. Even when not in bloom, these fast-growing trees are very decorative, and prefer it on the dry side when established. Hardy in Zone 9, iffy, but worth trying, with shelter, in Zone 8.

Caragana arborescens, Siberian pea shrub. Can grow quickly to tree size, about 20 feet. Ultra hardy, and very fast growing, if somewhat rank. Used in shelter belts in the Midwest. Lots of sweetly scented flowers in midsummer. Sort of a large-scale Scotch broom. Zone 2, or colder.

Citrus spp. Lemons, oranges, calamondins. Superb ornamentals, even if you don't live in Florida. The Orangery was a standard feature of any grand garden in the 18th and 19th centuries, wherein potted lemons and oranges would be moved for the winter. In the garden for the summer, the intermittent waves of white blossom perfume the air for a great distance. Small-growing Meyer lemon, calamondin, otaheite oranges, and kumquats are ideal for this treatment, and can make quite a centerpiece for an herb or rose garden. As a bonus, the leaves are fragrant when bruised, and can add a citrus flavor to food. Zone 9.

Cytisus battandieri, Atlas broom. A small tree with silvery compound leaves. In June, three-inch terminal clusters of light yellow flowers, scented of pineapple, adorn the branches. Prefers cooler summer areas, such as the Pacific Northwest. Hardy to Zone 7.

Elaeagnus angustifolia, Russian olive. Gorgeous silver-leaved tree with dramatically contrasting black bark for just about anywhere. Naturalized along watercourses in desert areas of the Great Basin and Columbia Plateau. Barely significant pale yellow flowers in early summer perfume a wide area. If you can't find a weeping silver-leaved pear to emulate Sissinghurst, this is just as fetching and a lot less trouble and expense. Zone 3, at least.

Magnolia spp. Our own *M. grandiflora* and *M. virginiana* are beautifully adapted to warm summer areas and their many cultivars, including *M.g.* 'Little Gem' (suitable for containers), ensure that just about anybody can grow one of these evergreen sorts. Their creamy white flowers scented of tea with lemon stud the dark green foliage intermittently from late spring to fall. Of the deciduous types the Asian *M. campbellii, M. sieboldii,* and *M. sprengeri* are probably best. Ivory and rose flowers, eight to ten inches across, cover the bare branches in early spring. They can take a long time to reach blooming size, but are doubtless worth the wait. Zone 7, but flower buds can be damaged by late cold spells.

Pittosporum undulatum, Victoria box. Another fast-growing Australian for frost-free locales. The evergreen three-inch leaves have rippled edges. Masses of white flowers, aging ivory, are borne periodically throughout the year. A light but rich scent, redolent of lemon peel, that carries well. And since they endure coastal conditions, there can be plenty of breeze to waft the scent. Zone 9.

Prunus spp. Plums and apricots. The musky-sweet scent is one of the first of the year. Fruiting plums, particularly of Japanese or American origin, also have the scent. *P. cerasifera, P.* x *blireiana* and other purple-leaved sorts are popular members of the group. *P. mume* from Japan is the first to bloom, often in January. The dozens of varieties grown in that country should find their way here eventually. Non-fruiting plums hardy to Zone 6, various fruiting plums hardy to Zone 1.

Robinia pseudoacacia, Black locust. Tall, rather unrefined trees with delicate compound pea foliage drip with clusters of wonderfully sweet white or pink flowers, reminiscent of *Wisteria.* Not for a formal garden, as they send up suckers from the roots. Try them in dry, rough areas particularly in the country in a no-nonsense grove. The roots fix nitrogen and the blossoms can be made into fritters. Varieties to be sought out (some, hybrids with magenta-flowering *R. viscosa*) are 'Idahoensis' and 'Decaisneana' with rose pink flowers, 'Pyramidalis' and 'Frisia' with chartreuse leaves, and 'Purple Robe' with purplish flowers and bronze new growth. Zone 3.

Styrax obassia, Fragrant snowbell. Sophisticated deciduous tree to 30 feet, with large rounded leaves. In June six-inch clusters of small white flowers hang from near the ends of branches. Good against an evergreen backdrop. Not always easy to find. Zone 5.

Tilia spp. Linden. Our native American linden, *T. americana,* has yellowish flowers, whereas *T. cordata* and *T.* x *euchlora* have whiter flowers. All are very sweetly scented and, dried, make a wonderful tea conjuring up images of June. Wonderful street and shade trees being quite tolerant of city pollution, but not noteworthy for autumn color. The American will do nicely in Zone 2, the others, in Zone 3.

Trees With Fragrant Foliage

Calocedrus decurrens, Incense cedar. Conifer native to mountains from Oregon to Baja California and widely adaptable. Flattened foliage like a *Thuja* (arborvitae) giving a sweet, resinous scent on warm days. Tolerant of poor soil and drought. Can be slow at first, but then fast to 70 feet. Zone 3.

Other conifers — *Thuja, Pinus, Juniperus, Cupressus.* Myriad varieties for all zones. Most release their scent, to varying degrees, when the weather is warm. All are fragrant when brushed against.

Eucalyptus spp. Australian gum. Australian genus of about 500 species, 150 of which have been grown from Arizona to British Columbia. Nearly all have some aromatic quality, the most noteworthy being *E. citriodora,* lemon-scented gum, *E. globulus,* blue gum (the most common), and *E. pulchella,* white peppermint gum. Zone 9. *E. gunnii* and *E. niphophila* are hardier to Zone 8.

Laurus nobilis, Grecian laurel. Broadleaved evergreen from which is obtained bay leaves. Dense and slow to 40 feet. Needs good drainage. Does well in pots anywhere. Small flowers in early summer are a sweet-scented bonus. Zone 8. Similar *Umbellularia californica* (California bay laurel, pepperwood, Oregon myrtle) has stronger scent. Zone 7 with some shelter.

Populus spp. Cottonwood, poplar, aspen. In spring, when the new leaves unfurl, they are coated with a sticky resin that has an unmistakable resinous, woodsy scent which carries for large distances. *P. balsamifera,* Balm of Gilead, is particularly good. These are "weed" trees, fast-growing but short-lived, and with horrible surface roots that sucker all over the place. But they're indispensable for country properties near ponds and streams or along lanes. One kind or another will grow in all zones.

Shrubs With Fragrant Flowers

From January to March not too much is doing in the garden, and we are particularly grateful for any signs of vitality. How gratifying that some of the sweetest fragrances appear at this time. Deciduous shrubs with similar requirements are witch hazel (*Hamamelis*) with yellow to orange fringe blossoms, Wintersweet (*Chimonanthus praecox*) bearing pale yellow waxen flowers, and winter hazel (*Corylopsis*) also with pale yellow flowers, but in hanging chains. All are rather slow growing, with open structure, and prefer a somewhat acid soil in a sheltered spot, to protect buds from cold snaps. Also of similar needs are *Viburnum* x *bodnantense* 'Dawn' and *Lonicera fragrantissima* (winter honeysuckle) with sparse clusters of rosy pink and white flowers respectively. Zone 7. *Mahonia bealei* and *M. japonica* are similar exotic-looking relatives of our Oregon grape, bearing shiny evergreen leaves that give them the look of a holly crossed with a palm tree. At the top of each stem are clusters of yellow flowers with a lily-of-the-valley scent. Zone 5. The sweet boxes *(Sarcococca* spp.) are all similarly unassuming dark green willowy broadleaved evergreens. *S. hookerana* var. *humilis* is a dwarf, wonderful for edging pathways, to about 18″. The others are all taller, to around three feet. The flowers are barely significant, but oh so fragrant. Particularly effective near entryways. Zone 7. A taller shrub, nearly a tree, is *Azara microphylla,* with a profusion of small fuzzy-looking white flowers scented of vanilla. Its graceful form and evergreen leaves are best displayed against a sheltering wall. Zone 8. As a group, the daphnes are some of the most fragrant of shrubs. The first to bloom is the rather gaunt *D. mezereum,* February daphne. Rosy purple or white flowers on leafless stems are followed by red or yellow berries. Zone 5. A bit later *D. odora* opens its rose-pink buds arranged in nosegays at the tips of its branches. The crystalline white flowers release a heady scent for yards around. Zone 7. Still later *D. cneorum,* rock daphne, smothers its neat, low-growing tuffets with deep pink flowers. Zone 7. In late spring, and intermittently thereafter, *D.* x *burk-* *woodii* 'Somerset' flowers along wandlike branches. Zone 5. Both *D. odora* and *D.* x *burkwoodii* have forms with white-edged leaves.

A bit later, in mid-spring, the Mexican orange *(Choisya ternata)* blooms. Bright, glossy evergreen leaves composed of three leaflets look top-notch year-round. And the masses of white flowers make a very clean appearance. The flowers have a delicate citrus fragrance, while the leaves have a sharp, but not unpleasant pungency. At about the same time, *Osmanthus delavayi* and x *Osmarea burkwoodii* come into bloom. They are quite similar, the latter being more or less a larger scale version of the former. Hordes of small white flowers, deliciously sweet, clothe the branches. The dark green, lustrous leaves are very handsome, and they both make wonderful hedges clipped or not. Zone 7. Another relative, *Osmanthus heterophyllus,* has hollylike leaves, but not so prickly. It blooms in the fall, filling the air with a gardenia scent. There are several varieties, some with variegated or purple leaves. Zone 5.

Another spring-blooming broadleaved evergreen creates mixed reactions in people. For some the romance of the Scottish Highlands is conjured up by Gorse *(Ulex europaeus).*

Buddleias are rank growers but if cut back in spring will produce a vigorous fountain of long blossom-tipped wands. Butterflies love them.

Calycanthus occidentalis, *spicebush, has four-inch leaves that smell of allspice and ginger. The flowers resemble narrow-petalled two-inch water lilies.*

Since a yellow pea flower or two can usually be found throughout the year, the saying arose that "when gorse is out of bloom, then kissing's out of fashion." During the main flush, the branches are wreathed in sweet blossoms, and it is quite a sight. But, in truth, there is hardly a spinier plant on earth, which makes it ideal for barrier plantings, but not much fun to garden around. Best left to rough places where it can mind itself. A double form also exists. Zone 6.

The genus *Rhododendron* contains a few fragrant members. Several eastern native species, such as *R. viscosum* (swamp azalea, Zone 4), *R. arborescens* (sweet azalea, Zone 5), and *R. prinophyllum* (roseshell azalea, Zone 3) offer delightful perfume. On the West Coast is *R. occidentale,* Zone 7. These and the Exbury and Mollis hybrids are all deciduous and all fragrant. Autumn foliage on some is exceptional. The evergreen cultivar 'Fragrantissimum' bears large blush-white flowers. Its lax habit makes it ideal for spilling over a wall or training as an espalier in Zone 9, or in a container elsewhere.

Other pea family members with fragrant yellow flowers are *Cytisus canariensis,* naturalized in coastal California, and *Spartium junceum,* Spanish broom. The former is less hardy, to about Zone 8, but flowers in mid-spring. Spanish broom gives a strong textural effect with its brushlike green nearly leafless branches. It also has the largest flowers of any of the brooms and one of the most pleasing perfumes. Zone 7.

The undisputed queen of spring-flowering shrubs is the lilac, *Syringa vulgaris.* There are dozens of varieties with single and double flowers from white through darkest purple. There's even a creamy-yellow variety called 'Primrose'. Some of the best are 'Charles Joly' (double red-violet), 'Ludwig Spaeth' (single dark purple), 'President Lincoln' (single wedgwood blue), and 'Sensation' (single wine red with white picotee edge). Not only are they hardy as can be, but they actually need cold to bloom well. Therefore, the Descanso hybrids were developed for warm-winter areas. The best known of these is 'Lavender Lady'. Unfortunately, once out of bloom, the shrubs have little to recommend them. Try encouraging a clematis or other vine to twine through. There are many other *Syringa* species, and hybrids derived from them, and, while beautiful to look at, most have a weedy smell, similar to the closely related privet.

Next in the seasonal procession are the mock oranges *(Philadelphus* spp.). We are willing to forgive their rather untidy growth for the sake of the ambrosial blossoms. Most bear white flowers, but 'Belle Etoile' has a rosy center. There are also doubles and dwarfs, and one with yellow foliage. Zone 2.

Now it's rose season. There are dozens of modern varieties with fragrant flowers, with names like 'Perfume Delight' and 'Fragrant Cloud', and these are not to be sneered at. But for a more useful form in the landscape, many of the older shrub roses are better, and even more fragrant. The hybrid rugosas are some of the sturdiest roses imaginable. They range in color from deep red-violet through pink to white, with 'Agnes' a lovely pale yellow. Their fragrance is nearly identical to the wild roses of ditches and hedgerows across America, and conjures up memories of country ramblings. As a testament to their durability, rugosas have naturalized on the dunes of Cape Cod. Another rose that has "gone wild," in some places to the point of pestiferousness, is *Rosa multiflora*. Left to its own devices, it becomes a billowing mound festooned with thousands of blush white-to-pink one-inch blossoms. With the aid of a tree to clamber in, or even a chain-link fence, it will hoist itself up to waft its fragrance far and wide. This is one of the few roses whose scent is "free on the air." And is it ever. It's a sweet, ladies' cosmetic sort of fragrance, reminding me of my mother's cold cream. Another sprawly shrub, excellent for training on a fence or wall, is the bright pink, thornless 'Zephirine Drouhin' also with very free scent. Much the same can be said of 'Sombreuil' which possesses the most unique flowers; creamy-white with a suggestion of palest flesh, its many petals looking as if someone sheared them off, flat, with a knife. The ancient apothecary's rose *(R. gallica)* has the distinction of actually having scented petals, so it is ideal for potpourri. And don't overlook the pink and rose striped version, 'Rosa Mundi'. 'Mme. Isaac Pereire' is regarded by many as the most fragrant of all old roses, but other candidates include the purple 'Charles de Mills', 'La France' (the first hybrid tea), 'Fantin Latour', 'Konigin von Danemark', 'Stanwell Perpetual', and 'Gruss an Aachen', the first floribunda. Some, but not all, of the hybrid musks possess a delicious fragrance, one of the best being 'Buff Beauty'. And a modern rose, 'The Yeoman' (one of the "English Roses" created by David Austin in the older

style), is redolent of that most elusive of rose scents, myrrh.

Rosa eglanteria, the sweetbriar, or Shakespeare's "Eglantine", bears single scentless flowers, but the foliage is fragrant of green apples particularly after a rain. So site this one where the prevailing south stormwinds will send its sweetness your way. In addition to having generally very fragrant flowers, the characteristic foliar protuberances that give moss roses their name possess scent glands. The scent is sweetly resinous and quite different from the blossoms.

Midsummer brings terminal clusters of small creamy flowers redolent of tea-with-lemon to *Pittosporum tobira* and its dwarf, cushion-forming variety, 'Wheeleri'. This broadleaved evergreen from Australia is hardy to Zone 8. Both standard and dwarf forms have variegated variants.

The many varieties of *Buddleia* bloom for weeks at this season. The nickname of summer lilac is appropriate both to the color range and the form of the inflorescence. Most widely adaptable are the tough-as-nails varieties of *Buddleia davidii* and its smaller counterpart, *B. davidii nanhoensis*. The latter's varieties are often marketed as 'Petite Plum' and 'Petite Indigo'. Other sorts, often hybrids with other species, are *B. fallowiana* varieties, and 'Lochinch', all with lovely gray leaves. All are rank growers, and if not cut back nearly to the ground annually in spring, make twiggy, coarse growth. But if this simple trick is practiced, a vigorous fountain of long blossom-tipped wands is produced, with clouds of gaudy butterflies hovering about; hence, the other common name of butterfly bush. Zone 4, at least.

Sweetpepper bush *(Clethra alnifolia)* is an August bloomer that prefers a damp site. Three-inch clusters of sparkling white blossoms waft their scent from the tips of the branches, and the pink flowered forms are to be sought out. Zone 3.

Shrubs With Fragrant Foliage
Many shrubs have leaves that reveal their fragrance when either sun-warmed or brushed

against. Rosemary and sage are two shrubs usually grown specifically for their fragrant leaves. Their many forms, both of stature and leaf color, warrant their use as ornamentals. Most are generally hardy to Zone 5, if good drainage and nutrient-poor soil are assured.

The spicebushes *(Calycanthus floridus* and *C. occidentalis)* have four-inch leaves redolent of allspice and ginger. The flowers are rather like narrow-petaled two-inch maroon waterlilies, having the substance of wood shavings. They have their own fragrance, often likened to strawberries. Zone 5.

In warmer areas hedges are often made of myrtle *(Myrtus communis)* as it is a very undemanding fine-textured plant that takes well to shearing. In colder areas it is often used for topiary accents in pots to be moved indoors for the winter. The fragrance is powerfully resinous, conjuring images of Italian formal gardens. Zone 8.

Cistus ladanifer and its hybrids proffer one of the most delightfully sweet fragrances on warm summer days. One looks about to see which flower is so fragrant, only to realize it's the dark green leaves of this rockrose. The common name derives from the two-inch white flowers, often with a ruby-red spot at the base of each petal. Individual crinkled-crepe blossoms are fleeting, but are borne in masses over a long season. Poor, dry soil assures hardiness to Zone 8.

Fragrant Vines

Much has been made of late of the kiwi vines, *Actinidia* spp., for their fruiting virtues. *A. arguta* bears its gooseberry-size fruit to at least Zone 4. Its relative, *A. kolomikta,* equally hardy, is a sought-after ornamental grown for its masses of velvety leaves, tipped with white and bright pink. But both of these have deliciously fragrant flowers, particularly towards evening. Plant them near a bedroom window or terrace to take full advantage of this quality. But beware — cats can ravage a newly planted vine in a frenzy induced by the plant, much as with catnip.

The clematis tribe contains some fragrant-flowered members. The showers of straw-

yellow bells of *C. rehderiana,* Zone 5, and the foaming white masses of *C. dioscoreifolia,* Zone 6, scent the air of summer and early autumn. In Zone 7, the evergreen *C. armandii* fills the air with orange blossom scent in early spring. There are white and pale pink flowered versions. Some clones of *C. montana* have a decided vanilla aroma, but this varies from plant to plant.

Some of the honeysuckles are noxious weeds in certain parts of the country. *Lonicera japonica* can get out of hand, but where it behaves, its all-summer perfume is a delight. Making more of a visual impact is *L. periclymenum* and its varieties and hybrids. The rose or scarlet and cream-yellow flowers are borne in great profuse clusters. Zone 3.

The jasmines are the quintessential fragrant vines. *Jasminum sambac, J. polyanthum,* and *J. nitidum* are, alas, for Zone 9. But poet's jasmine, *J. officinale* and its pink-flowered hybrid *J.* x *stephanense* will grow, with summer heat and winter protection, in Zone 7. *J. polyanthum* also makes a delightful hanging basket subject for a cool greenhouse, blooming in February. Of a similar nature, Confederate jasmine, *Trachelospermum jasminoides* is commonly used as a ground cover, but will climb modestly. It's scent can be a bit on the cloying side. Zone 8, with shelter.

Many of the climbing sports of modern bedding roses are rather stiff things, bearing their blossoms in a manner more appropriate to the shrubs from which they arose. Their flowers are often both sparse and non-recurrent, and can have the perplexing habit of facing up, which is fine for the sparrows, but not so good for mere mortals looking from below. However, many of the older roses have gracefully nodding flowers, perched in a fashion that not only lets us see the flowers, but invite a good, deep sniff. 'Etoile de Hollande', 'Lady Forteviot'. and 'La France' are sports of older hybrid teas that possess charm as well as the required fragrance. 'Belle Portugaise' and 'Dr. W. van Fleet' will clothe the ugliest of buildings with huge masses of flowers. The generous 'Doctor' has an even more generous sport,

'New Dawn', identical in every way except for the fact that its trusses of lovely pink flowers are borne all season–particularly lovely with one of the Dutch honeysuckles. The white form of *Rosa banksiae* has a scent of violets, very early in the season, but is rather tender, chancy even in Zone 8. *R. soulieana,* however is hardy to at least Zone 3, and its incredible profusion of white flowers fills the air with a honey scent. Several lax-growing ramblers derived from *R. arvensis* were developed in Scotland, and bear the generic name Ayrshire Ramblers. Their two-inch loosely double flowers festoon remarkably healthy and vigorous vinelike canes, even in nearly full shade — wonderful for covering old eyesores, or for adding another dimension to rhododendron grottoes. 'Ayrshire Splendens' is an available variety, and it is sweetly fragrant.

The wisterias are as generous with their scent as they are of blossom. The shorter-clustered *W. sinensis* and *W. venusta* varieties, as well as the elegant, ethereal three-foot clusters of *W. floribunda* all perfume the air deliciously. Zone 4.

Several lesser-known plants offer alternatives to this list of tried-and-true vines. *Anredera cordifolia,* Madeira vine, forms tubers that can be dug and stored over winter in cold areas. The main requirement for production of its foot-long, white flower clusters is heat.

Chilean jasmine, *Mandevilla laxa,* is an all-too-rarely-seen gem hardy to Zone 7. Clusters of two-inch white gardenia-scented trumpets are borne most of the summer.

The passion vines all bear exotic or bizarre flowers, and at least one of them, *Passiflora alatocaerulea,* adds fragrance to the effect. The orange egg-shaped fruit is both ornamental and edible. Zone 7.

In sub-tropical regions, *Stephanotis floribunda* bears its waxen white bells, which most of us only see in bridal bouquets. It can also be grown to great effect in a warm greenhouse.

A native-American member of the pea family, *Apios americana,* is valued mostly for its freely produced edible tubers, which, historically, helped sustain many a Pilgrim forefather. However, the clusters of rosy blossoms are also very fragrant, reminiscent of violets. Zone 3.

And no list of vines would be complete without that other member of Leguminosae, the sweet pea. Although an annual, with coaxing it can reach ten feet or more. The range of colors is wonderful, as is the profligacy of bloom. A cool summer area and very frequent picking of blooms are best for ensuring a long season of sweetness. ✑

Sources

Roses of Yesterday and Today
802 Brown's Valley Rd.
Watsonville, CA. 95076

Forestfarm
990 Tetheral Rd.
Williams, OR. 97544
A wonderful assortment of woody things, some quite unusual.

Lamb Nursery
E. 101 Sharp Ave.
Spokane, WA. 99202
Mostly perennials, but vines and shrubs, too.

Wayside Gardens
Hodges, SC 29695
Large listing of first-class plants of all descriptions.

Pickering Nurseries, Inc.
670 Kingston Rd.
Pickering, Ontario, LIV 1A6
Canada
Extensive list of all types of roses. Catalog $2.

Fragrant Houseplants

Lorraine Kiefer

Hybrid lilies are a real challenge for indoor gardeners. 'Casa Blanca' has large spectacular flowers that are very fragrant.

Photos by Lorraine Kiefer

Candles, potpourri, and simmer pots can all add fragrance to a room. My favorite way, however, is the natural way — with a window full of fragrant plants.

If you have a window that receives a few hours of sunlight a day, you can grow one or more of the fragrant plants that will bloom indoors. Fragrant plants bring a new dimension to a windowsill of green plants. A fresh, springlike fragrance is a joy on a snowy day! Some plants such as the sweet olive (*Osmanthus fragrans*) are very easy to grow and bloom most of the year. Others, such as paperwhite narcissus or hyacinth, have a much shorter time of bloom, but are intensely fragrant and colorful.

There are many types of fragrant plants from which to choose. Before deciding which plants are for you, consider these factors. First, approximate the hours of sunlight at each window in which you could place the plants. Also determine which areas are cool and which are near heat sources. Many fragrant plants need a cool place in order to bloom. Others, like jasmine, need a warm, humid area, often found in a laundry room, kitchen, or shower area. Very few will flourish in a dry, warm spot, but I have found that a hoya bloomed riotously in a west window near a fireplace. One warning: some folks find that a blooming hoya is really too sweet in a small room.

Lorraine Kiefer and her husband Ted own and operate Triple Oaks Nursery and Florist in Franklinville, New Jersey. Her special interests are herbs, fragrant plants, wildflowers, and perennials. Lorraine writes garden columns for the Franklin Twp. Sentinel *and* Jersey Woman, *and she is a frequent contributor to the* Green Scene.

There are a few common sense rules to follow for success with most plants, including the fragrant ones. I have found that all need fresh air and fairly cool temperatures, especially at night. Good light is important, but there are certain plants that will adjust to less light and still flower. A good, well-drained potting soil such as Pro Mix is safe and easy to use. Most houseplant fertilizers are fine when used as directed or even diluted a little bit more than recommended. I usually stop feeding all my plants at Halloween and don't start again until the New Year; during the dark days of December the plants don't need as much food, although a plant in active bloom in strong sun will benefit from half-strength fertilizer once during this period.

It is important to find the right spot for each fragrant plant. I can grow fragrant olive everywhere in my house where there is a window, including places that only get a brief kiss of morning sunlight. On the other hand, jasmine is much more selective.

Jasmine *(Jasminum sambac)*, a native of India, is a wonderfully fragrant vine that needs a warm, sunny spot when grown indoors. It will take partial shade while outdoors for the summer. It loves humidity, which can be created by pans of pebbles filled with water under plants in sunny bay windows. Grow the jasmine in a hanging basket above the other plants and keep it cut back and fed so it looks healthy and bushy. A stringy-looking jasmine probably needs trimming, food, and more light. A summer outdoors will usually remedy any health problem.

There are many types of jasmine. Most require the kind of care outlined above, but some may bloom more readily than others. I feel that if I am going to have a hanging basket or a vine, it might as well be a jasmine. It is really worth growing jasmines because of their delightful fragrance.

Another vine that is both beautiful and fragrant is the passiflora or passion flower. Some varieties are more fragrant than others, and all have wonderful flowers. I first saw the plant many years ago, while honeymooning in Bermuda where there is a passion flower perfume factory. Since then I have grown many of these lovely plants successfully, both on a porch in the summer and in a sunny bay window in winter. They do best in hanging pots unless you are willing to trellis them or allow the vines to climb around a window. They will only flower when it is warm, but can tolerate cool temperatures during their winter rest period. I find that cutting my plants back during the winter encourages good growth and blooming in the late spring, summer and fall. Don't hesitate to prune these vines anytime if they look lanky. Like other heavy-blooming tropicals, they can be fed weekly from March to October with a mild liquid fertilizer.

Another great family of fragrant plants is the citrus, including the lemon, orange, lime, and grapefruit. All can be obtained in a dwarf form, and they grow very well in most cool homes. I have grown them all in almost all of my windows. They do well as long as it's not too hot and dry; citrus drop their leaves in rooms where there are woodstoves or fireplaces. A summer outdoors usually revives these plants, especially if they are well watered. They will grow in sun or light shade when outdoors, feed twice a month. If the plants are outdoors in the summer, natural pollination can take place, and they will produce colorful fruit. The flowers bloom for a very long season and at times are so numerous they actually make a mess when the petals drop. I find their wonderful, old-fashioned fragrance well worth the trouble of sweeping up a few petals. Many times my trees have had both blooms and fruit at the same time, making them both colorful and fragrant.

A fairly unusual plant, *Clerodendrum fragrans,* is bushy, with roselike flowers borne in large double white clusters. Like many blooming plants, these plants need good light, but not direct sun. Pinch back all the time, and cut back drastically in February since blossoms only occur on new growth. These plants need a lot of water during the blooming season, but they also need good drainage.

Another real challenge, but one that I have had great success with, is the *Stephanotis.* This is a wonderful climber with sweetly scented, waxy white flowers. Called the wedding flower by many, this plant blooms with large clusters of blossoms if kept in a warm, sunny spot. In the winter I like to keep my plant in a western bay window in my dining room where it has lots of moisture from other plants and sun all day. The vine often has to be cut back to keep it from tangling with the hanging jasmines. In the summer this plant goes on the porch, right next to my front door, where it gets morning sun only, and lots of moisture. I was thrilled when clusters of fragrant blooms appeared to greet all who came to my door.

Although more popular, the gardenia is not as easy to grow as the sweet olive and jasmine. The gardenia that is commonly found in the home is *G. jasminoides,* named because of its jasminelike scent. Gardenias require cool nights and sunny days — the more sun, the more flowers. If the plant has less than four hours of sunlight, it will probably not form buds. Although the gardenia can tolerate hot days, night temperatures must not go over 60 degrees if it is to set buds. It also needs constant moisture and high humidity. A tray or dish of pebbles, such as those used in fish tanks, can be placed under the plant and kept full of water. In addition, gardenias need a lot of acid, and they will become yellow if the pH is too alkaline. Remember the grandmothers who poured left-over tea into the gardenias? They were unknowingly lowering the pH. Summer them outdoors, especially during the humid days. Buds that set during the cool evenings of spring will swell in the humidity and bloom.

If you have a hard time getting a gardenia to bloom, there is a gardenia relative that is a lot easier to grow, although it is a bit more difficult to locate — African gardenia *Mitriostigma axillare.* The blooms are arbutus shaped and fragrant.

Some of the plants grown outside in temperate regions can be grown as houseplants in the north. Sometimes it is difficult to locate these plants, but they can be found. One I especially like is the *Daphne odora,* a shrub with fragrant pink flowers that can be grown in a cool window.

Many of the fragrant plants that you might want to include in your indoor garden do not have conspicuous flowers. Some, such as the scented geranium, are grown for the fragrance of their leaves rather than their flowers. One that is not exciting looking has very fragrant leaves, patchouli (*Pogostemon patchouli*). This plant provides oil for one of the oldest known perfumes, and in ancient times linen from India was scented with patchouli. Place in a very warm spot and provide lots of water. I have had good luck growing it in my western exposure bay window. The plant responds to the lightest touch by releasing its heady, rather mysterious fragrance. Since ancient times its leaves have been harvested, dried, and packed in bales for export to places that make oil of patchouli.

One of my favorite fragrant plants is rosemary. It is not easy to grow indoors if the house is warm and dry, but rosemary will flourish in unheated sunrooms, window-well gardens, and very cool bay windows. Although rosemary prefers well-drained soil when grown outdoors, it is wise to flush water through its soil often when it is grown indoors. It is also important to give the plant lots of sun or the fragrance will not be as strong and the growth will be weak. My plants flourish in an unheated plant room that has sunlight all day and cool temperatures at night. They are especially beautiful during the winter when they bloom. Shakespeare said, "Rosemary for remembrance." Once you've touched this marvelous plant and enjoyed its unique odor, you'll never forget it! It is often used for cooking, bathing, potpourri, and decorations.

Some plants like the star anise grow as easily as ficus, which they resemble, and they have a great spicy aroma. Star anise becomes a large tree in tropical areas such as Java, but it will adapt to the average house if given fairly good light and water. Indigenous to China and North Vietnam, it has long been used as a spice in India, but it was not known in Europe until the mid 1500s. In the wild it is usually found in sunny high areas where the soil retains moisture. Although the flowers and pods are not showy, the pods are aromatic and the leaves are very pleasant smelling, as indicated by the name, *Illicium* (which means "that which entices from the very pleasant scent of the tree and fruit").

A houseplant that has fragrant flowers and dainty leaves is common myrtle, *Myrtus communis.* This is a very popular plant in southern Europe, where its leaves are used in cooking, medicines, cosmetics, and wedding decorations.

The plants discussed so far have all been long-lived plants, many of which grow to tree size in their native environments. Another group that can bring wonderful fragrances to the indoors are the many plants grown from bulbs. Most of these have to be planted while dormant and given a cool period to form roots before they will bloom. Some bulbs such as hyacinths and paperwhite narcissus can often be purchased precooled. Once green shoots are showing on any type of bulb plant it is time to move it into strong light where temperatures are cool. Temperatures that are too high will cause weak, lanky growth and poor bloom.

Several types of narcissus and miniature daffodils will delight you with their springlike fragrances and color. Some iris and tulips are also fragrant.

It is a challenge to try the magnificent hybrid lilies. 'Star Gazer' and 'Rubrum' both have showy pink-and-white blooms and are fragrant. The 'Casablanca' lily has much larger and more spectacular flowers that are also fragrant. Pot the bulbs in late fall or very early spring and place in a cool spot. After good roots have formed, move to a cool window, greenhouse window, or plant room.

'Star Gazer' and 'Rubrum' lilies both have showy pink and white blossoms. Pot bulbs in the fall or early spring and place in cool spot. When rooted, move to a cool window.

Freesias can enliven the late winter or early spring window with their fragrance. Not the easiest plants to grow, they should be started in a very cool spot that is above freezing. I usually plant mine between Halloween and Thanksgiving and place them in my hobby greenhouse. Only a shallow container, like a bulb pot, is necessary. I stake the grasslike foliage. Stems will be weak if the light is not good or if there is too much nitrogen in the fertilizer. Remember that these plants need good light in order to produce blooms in 10 to 12 weeks.

Lilies-of-the-valley can be lifted from the garden just before they break through the soil. Place them in an attractive container in moist potting soil. Water well and keep in a cool, bright window until the blooms appear.

Besides the bulbs and shrub-type plants, there are other fragrant plants. One worth mention is the night blooming cereus. My original plant came from a cutting from an elderly couple who had a plant in a pot the size of a bushel basket. I started it and forgot about it. Each summer it went out on the porch, each winter it went wherever there was room. Some years the unsightly plant even went into an attic room where it was often cold and where I usually neglected to water it.

One summer we noticed several very large buds. We watched daily as they seemed to swell with the heat and humidity characteristic of our southern New Jersey Julys. One dusk we noticed the unbelievable fragrance of this bud and realized that it would probably bloom that evening. Soon we had assembled a group of people, including the editor of the small weekly where I write a garden column. Chilled white wine and a beautiful summer evening made a great setting for the debut of this fragrant flower. It was worth the wait and truly an unexpected treat. I can best describe the bloom as a huge white tropical bird ready to fly. The fragrance was a potpourri of all the lilies I have ever enjoyed. The next morning it was gone. There were other blooms that summer, and summers to come, but none as large and magnificent as that first.

Another spectacular bloomer with lovely white blooms is the Amazon lily, *Eucharis grandiflora*. This handsome green plant resembles other popular tropicals and will thrive with good moisture and light. I have found that when my plants are put out under a lath roof for the summer and left there until just before frost they flower profusely in the cold months. They usually start blooming around Thanksgiving and continue most of the winter. Unlike the bulbs, these plants remain foliage plants most of the time, with only a brief resting period after blooming, when less water is required.

Some plant varieties are more fragrant than others. The oleander, *Nerium oleander* is an example — it is most fragrant. Given plenty of moisture and sun, with lots of food during the warm months, this one will add fragrance to your patio all summer and then perfume the indoors during the autumn as long as it receives good light.

There are many good books on fragrant plants. You may also want to visit botanical gardens and actually smell these plants, since fragrances often provoke very subjective responses.

Remember that *fragrans, odorata,* and *-osme* in a name usually indicate that the plant has fragrance. Also bear in mind that the amount of light, the temperature, and the amount of fertilizer will all have an effect on the fragrance.

Once the fragrant indoor garden is established it is important to follow certain guidelines. Humidity is very important. No matter where the plants are located, water must be near by. Try adding an attractive garden fountain or a birdbath if space and decor permit. A fish tank helps provide moisture, as well as bowls of water with colorful pebbles.

Jasmine is a wonderfully fragrant vine that needs a warm, sunny spot when grown indoors. It will grow in partial shade outdoors in summer.

Frequent baths can help control insects. This takes time, but it is an enjoyable way to "be with" your fragrant plants. I sometimes shower my plants right after I do the dishes, leaving them to drain all night before putting them back in the window. This also allows me time to wipe off the sill and any other areas that could harbor insects.

I use a systemic insecticide in the soil of all the plants that summer outdoors. The systemic, taken into the system of the plant, makes the leaves distasteful and poisonous to insects. I find this treatment safer than sprays, which get all over me and the house as well as the plant. I do use sprays when the insects can be seen, but I take the plant to the porch or garage before spraying. Always follow directions and spread a spoonful of potting soil around the plant to eliminate any odor.

With minimal care, moderate-to-good light and common sense, you can successfully grow most fragrant plants. They will add color, fragrance and a hint of spring to your indoor garden. ❧

Recommended Reading

The Avant Gardener, 1988, *Horticultural Data Processors,* New York, NY, Vol. 20, No. 11.

Helen Van Pelt Wilson and Leonie Bell, *The Fragrant Year,* M. Barrows & Co., NY, 1967.

SCENTED GERANIUMS, MIMIC PLANTS

Clorinda

Bertha Reppert

Believe it or not, here in cold Zone 6, on my winter windowsill, I can grow a profusion of exotics — ginger, nutmeg, orange, rose, peppermint, apple, cinnamon, pine, apricot and more, much more. It's my scented geranium collection, mimic plants, that come in all these glorious fragrances and flavors.

My first encounter was with a common rose geranium, a slip given by a neighbor that rooted easily in water and then grew like Jack's beanstalk, quickly filling an entire sunny south window. It seems I spent that winter repotting my eager-to-grow houseplant, ruffling its fragrant leaves every time I passed by. As a young bride, flexing new found green thumbs, I found it an amazing acquisition, certainly memorable.

Since then, I have never been without a rose geranium in the garden or on the windowsill. Enthusiastic collecting has added dozens of additional scented geraniums to the collection. I am hooked on the unexpected "hidden virtues" of these tantalizing aromatic plants.

Although everyone calls them geraniums, they are properly pelargoniums, denizens of the southern hemisphere that have irregular flowers in two and three petal groups and an adnate nectar tube. Since these ancient plants were first discovered in South Africa in the 17th century and brought to England by botanist John Tradescant, they have been called "sweet geraniums." And indeed they are in the family Geraniaceae, along with the true geranium species, plants hardy in temperate zones.

Within the realm of herbs, the scented geraniums are a specialty unto themselves. No fragrance garden dares to be without its specimen rose or lemon or peppermint geranium in the beds or as accent plants in large containers.

Amenable to either situation, these heat lovers are especially adaptable to container culture, making splendid patio plants. Grouped in collections of varied leaf forms,

---

Bertha Reppert, author of A Heritage of Herbs *(Stackpole Books, 1976) owns a herb and spice shop, Rosemary House, in Mechanicsburg, Pennsylvania.*

textures, sizes and appealing scents, they are among the most desirable of potted landscape features, especially on a hot humid summer day when the leaves automatically release their oils into the air.

Given reasonable soil, good drainage and as much sun as possible, scented geraniums reward their growers with everything except flowers. Of course they do flower (and a certain few have spectacular blooms) but they do not produce the great balls of color found on the geraniums commonly used as bedding plants. Although some flowering occurs all year-round, the best bloom is in the garden in summer.

It is not only what you see you get with these lovelies—it's their astonishing fragrance that sets them apart, a built-in aroma released at a touch. Caress them all you like . . . they love to be petted.

Since these natural air refreshers are also edible, they can be enjoyed on the menu as well as for perfume in the air. Parties indoors or out are doubly enhanced by lemon, spice, eucalyptus, coconut, lime, almond, and strawberry to say nothing of assorted pungent fragrances from the many hybrid combinations of all of the above. Helen Van Pelt Wilson writes "The scent of geraniums isn't a subject for logical argument at all, only a cause of delight."

Lady Plymouth

It will amuse your guests to rub the leaves, release the volatile oils, then guess their names. For instance, 'Clorinda' has been described as lemon, nutmeg or eucalyptus scented. I call it spicy. However, discreetly placed labels are helpful aids to learning the "Who's Who" of scented geraniums. I put name tags on all my potted collections, for my benefit as well as for others.

Children are fascinated by these imitators. Given furred peppermint leaves to pet or teeny tiny lemon leaves with their distinctive strong odors, the surprise engenders priceless reactions. The haunting fragrance will linger on their hands for some time.

Planted directly in open soil, most scented geraniums soon grow to enormous proportions. In the Washington D.C. area two feet is not unusual; in California or Florida they easily reach four feet tall and wide. All of the foliage is useful; gather bunches for use indoors, to carry, or to distribute to everyone you know as charming scented nosegays.

Where they are tender, cut back the tops (a harvest to be dried or rooted) and root prune before repotting the plants and returning them to winter quarters indoors. Do this a month or so before you plan to bring them inside. As perennials, they will rest a while before setting forth new growth.

In the sunny south where temperatures do not fall below 20 degrees these tender perennials can be left outside. Willing to tolerate occasional frost, they will easily weather light snows. Under tropical conditions, they become subshrubs.

Although mine never achieve shrub proportions, I enjoy my winter windowsill coterie. It's quite true what they say about "aromatherapy" — they lift my spirits on the dreariest of days. To touch them is to love them.

They reside and perform in every light situation available, including grow lights of any sort. Although they do better in the sunniest window, where they will delight you with flowers, they will endure, though growth will be spindly, in north light. Good drainage and careful watering seem to be their most rigorous demands. Occasional feeding with any good houseplant fertilizer (I use Peters, fish emulsion or Electra) and pinching back weak growth, which can be used for little boutonnieres, will keep them happy.

Careless watering will do in a geranium more quickly than neglect. Since watering is a variable — depending upon the size of the pot, the porosity of the soil, the needs of the plant, and the heat and humidity in the room — it's difficult to give explicit directions.

Feel the soil with your fingers — water when dry. Much of my collection is housed on a large tray of wet pebbles, and, although it is not portable, it holds a good many plants seeking moisture as needed.

I also like to "double pot" larger plants — a clay pot inside an old crock or cachepot with a few styrofoam packing peanuts in the bottom. Indoors these rarely need water more than once a week even in full sun.

Recycle those packing peanuts as excellent drainage in the bottoms of large containers. Sterile and lightweight, they protect the roots from the danger of rotting in standing water while reducing the weight of large pots considerably.

I also cover the drainage holes with old nylons. This effectively retains the loose soil while repelling pesky insects that sometimes make their homes in pot bottoms.

A basket of flowers of scented geraniums shows the variety of colors and the combination of colors of some scented geraniums.

'Mrs. Taylor' is a good candidate for a sunny window. It flowers freely and its leaves are scented.

Although occasionally one of the collection leaves me for whatever reason, these agreeable houseplants are not particularly prone to insects or diseases. The heavy oils may well be repellent. They are simply short-lived perennials. When I lose one, I gather up all the dried leaves, which continue to live on in the next potpourri mixture.

Pelargoniums are best started from cuttings; however, a few grow readily from seed. Apple-scented with its clusters of insignificant flowers, frequently self-sows outdoors, popping up in unexpected places. In fact, it sometimes refuses to start from cuttings, especially those taken from its trailing stems, as all the others do so willingly. Take cuttings from the outside shoots at the base of the plant with a bit of the base if possible.

Coconut-scented is another obliging self-sower, and little plants often can be found nestling around the mother plant.

To start geraniums, take soft cuttings either in early spring from succulent growth or in fall from firmer stalks. Avoid mature wood. Three-to-six-inch cuttings cut straight across, dipped in rooting hormone and inserted into damp coarse sand, perlite, vermiculite, or even potting soil will give you vigorous new plants for the garden or to use as gifts. They root in three to six weeks, usually faster in fall, but they can be contrary and take longer.

Professionals recommend hardening off geranium cuttings in the air for a day before attempting to root them. It is also wise to remove all bottom leaves as these will rot underground before rooting takes place. Strong overhead light, gentle bottom heat (about 60 degrees) and careful misting assure success. Scented geraniums are so easy to propagate that a collection can easily proliferate into a small business if you are so inclined.

A potful of dampened sand will support a dozen cuttings. Pop it into a closed plastic bag for several weeks and no extra care is necessary. Put your cuttings in a north light lest the heat build-up inside the plastic cook them. In full sun I have seen temperatures rise to 120 degrees in such a set-up. Once they are rooted, move them into strong light gradually.

Sometimes I simply plunge my good-sized piece of stalk into a colored glass of water where it roots readily in several weeks. An unexpected aid to this casual method is a small piece of pussy willow. As the willow thrusts out its water roots (and it will) the water becomes filled with natural rooting hormones that encourage the geranium to root. This amazing "willow water" will put roots on begonia slips, African violet leaves, and even tough old woody pieces of rosemary — much to my amazement. Try it.

Plant your rooted cuttings in a mixture of potting soil. I use half Pro-Mix combined with half vermiculite, perlite or sharp sand. Thus lightened, the soil provides the good drainage geraniums prefer.

Although they like to be on the dry side, watch carefully for wilting, then water. A filled

This rose-scented geranium has delightful red flowers and attractive foliage.

watering can keeps the water at room temperature and excess chlorine will have escaped into the air. Besides, our four-legged housepets find it handy.

The cuttings will soon graduate into larger pots, some eventually reaching tub size. Plan on repotting the robust geraniums several times for maximum size. A pinhead of vitamin B_1 to a quart of water lessens the trauma of transplanting. Do this especially with young rooted cuttings or those just received in the mail.

A spectacular hanging basket may hold several plants for full effect. Remember, this requires watering more often as well as frequent feedings for continued vigor. Bear in mind, however, that over-fertilizing or too-rich soil results in oversized growth with reduced fragrance. To intensify fragrance, give the scented plants an occasional dose of Epsom Salts, one cup to a gallon of water.

Topiaries have suddenly taken the potted plant world by storm. Certain scented geraniums lend themselves to this creative art form. 'Old Fashioned Rose', 'Clorinda', 'Rollinson's Unique', 'Pungent Peppermint', 'Giant Oak' and 'Old Scarlet Unique' can become imposing five-foot lollipop plants when trained successfully. The "crispum" group of treelike lemon geraniums make somewhat smaller specimens, equally charming.

Unless you already have a very tall plant available, select long cuttings from your stock plants, the longest, straightest and most vigorous shoots available. Do not pinch out the tops as you wish to encourage upright growth.

Take as many cuttings as you wish, then add a few extras as insurance. As soon as they root, pot them in individual four-inch pots of amended houseplant soil to which has been added a cup of bonemeal to a gallon of soil.

As a plant grows, remove bottom and lateral shoots only, forcing top growth until your standard is as tall as desired. Only then can the top be pinched out to encourage bushiness.

Along the way you will be increasing pot size and, very important, staking the little tree-to-be with a sturdy dowel. Do you envision a three-foot standard or a five-foot standard? Use the size stake necessary to support your plant, firmly anchored and securely tied to the trunk lest the brittle stalk snap in an ill wind.

In the second year, your pride should be blooming atop its tall stalk, flourishing on its own. Such handsome additions to the collection, worthy of a proper jardiniere, will surely stand out in the crowd. With proper care it will give you years of pleasure.

Not usually grown for their sometimes wispy flowers, the strong essential oils captured in pelargonium leaves have been one of the most important fragrance ingredients for commercial purposes. The perfume industry utilizes tons of geranium oil from leaves and stems, a substitute for costly rose oil. In the 1800s England established rose geranium plantations in South Africa for distillation purposes.

In these mimic plants, the fragrance quickly translates into flavor. Enjoy them as sweet-scented bouquets, potpourris, fireplace incense, or sachets but also try them in your cuisine.

A few leaves in a sugar bowl impart a subtle flavor; toss a leaf of peppermint or lemon into your next pot of tea; a few of the flowers deliciously grace any dessert; chop some leaves into your next tossed salad; float a pretty leaf in your breakfast orange juice; or freeze the leaves in ice cubes for festive goblets of water; serve a salad on the largest leaves in your collection; wrap butter in the largest fresh rose geranium leaves for a day or two while the fat extracts the oils with the magnetic affinity of enfleurage.

Experiment with all the flavors found in scented geraniums. You will enjoy your fragrant houseplants all the more. Oh, yes, the Victorians doted on tiny lemon geranium leaves in their finger bowls. Try that bit of fun on your next dinner guests.

Caution: To start a collection of these easy going aromatic and edible herbs is to want them all! It's exactly like dipping into a box of assorted chocolates; one can't stop. Be warned, it's more than just another hobby.

The search for new and different "SCENTEDS" is half the fun. The rewards lie in the astounding variations within the collection. One would need an enormous window to house them all. No one greenhouse has them all; here are some sources to explore. ❧

SOURCES

Merry Gardens
P. O. Box 595, Camden, ME 04843
(Catalog $1.00)

Catnip Acres Herb Farm
Christian Street, Oxford, CT 06483

Shady Hill Gardens
821 Walnut St., Batavia, IL 60510

Logee's Greenhouses
55 North Street, Danielson, CT 06239
(Catalog $3.00)

Sandy Mush Herb Farm
Rt. 2, Surrett Cave Rd., Leicester, NC 28748

Fox Hill Farm
444 W. Michigan Ave., Box 7, Parma, MI 49269

Well-Sweep Herb Farm
317 Mt. Bethel Road, Port Murray, NJ 07865

The Rosemary House
120 S. Market St., Mechanicsburg, PA 17055
(Catalog $2.00)

Caprilands Herb Farm
534 Silver Street
Coventry, CT 06238
(List for SASE)

Young's Mesa Nursery
2755 Fowler St., Arroyo Grande, CA 93420
(Catalog $2.00 refundable)

Cook's Geranium Nursery
712 N. Grand St., Lyons, KS 67554
(Catalog $1.00 refundable)

Abbreviated List of Scented Geraniums

Rose Scents
Attar of Roses
Giant Rose
Grey Lady Plymouth
Lady Plymouth (*P. graveolens*)
Old Fashioned Rose
Rober's Lemon Rose

Silverleaf Rose
Dr. Livingston
Snowflake
Velvet Rose

Minty Scents
Chocolate Mint
Joy Lucille
Mrs. Kingsley
Peppermint (*P. tomentosum*)
Pungent Peppermint (*P. denticulatum*)
Variegated Mint
Peppermint Rose

Spicy Scents
Cinnamon
Cody's Nutmeg
Ginger (*P. 'Toronto'*)
Old Spice
Pretty Polly

Pungent Scents
Brilliant
Fern Leaf (*P. denticulatum* 'Filicifolium')
Gooseberry
Oak Leaf

Lemon Scents
Crispum (*P. crispum*)
Lemon Balm (*P. x mellissinum*)
Lime
Limoneum
Prince Rupert
French Lace
Mabel Grey

Fruity Scents
Apricot (*P. scabrum*)
Prince of Orange
Apple (*P. odoratissimum*)
Coconut (*P. grossularioides*)
Strawberry
Fruity

Specialty Scents
Pine (*P. denticulatum*)
Filbert (*P. x concolor*)
Scarlet Unique
Clorinda

Free Flowering Scented
Clorinda
Crow's Foot

Mrs. Taylor
Scarlet Unique
Filbert
Prince of Orange
Shrubland Rose
Brilliant
Capri
Fair Ellen (*P. quercifolium*)
Staghorn Oak

BIBLIOGRAPHY

Staff of L.H. Bailey Hortorium.
Hortus Third, Cornell University, Macmillan Publishing Co., N.Y.C.

Helen Van Pelt Wilson. *Geraniums/ Pelargoniums for Window and Garden,* M. Barrows and Co., Inc., N.Y.C. 1946

Helen Noyes Webster. *Herbs: How to Grow Them and How to Use Them,* Charles T. Branford Co., Publisher: 1939

Jill Jesse. *The Perfume Album,* Perfume Perfections Press: 1951

Abbie Zabor. *The Potted Herb,* Stewart, Tabor and Chang: 1988

Audrey O'Connor and Mary Hirshfield. *An Herb Garden Companion,* Published by Cornell Plantations

Madeline Hill and Gwen Barkley (with Jean Hardy). Phyllis Shaudys. *The Pleasure of Herbs,* A Garden Way Book: 1987

Here's one I just heard about, haven't seen it yet — David Clark. *Kew Gardening Guide to Pelargoniums,* English

Peggie Schulz. *All About Geraniums,* Doubleday & Co. Inc. Garden City, N. Y. 1965

Jan Taylor. *Geraniums and Pelargoniums; The Complete Guide to Cultivation, Preparation and Exhibition,* Crowood Press/David & Charles 1988

In pursuit of the elusive Pelargonium, contact THE INTERNATIONAL GERANIUM SOCIETY (Dues $12.50 yearly) 4610 Druid Street, Los Angeles, CA 90032

Night Music

Tovah Martin

My work often keeps me in the greenhouse after dark. Suddenly, that familiar place takes on an entirely different character. Shapes loom awkwardly and leafy branches block my path. The greenhouse becomes a strange, new world.

It's well worth staying after the sun goes down. Bright colors that took center stage by day blend into the shadows after dark and white blossoms pop out in the moonlight. The

Tovah Martin is the staff horticulturist at Logee's Greenhouses in Danielson, Connecticut. She is also a freelance writer and the author of Once Upon a Windowsill: A History of Indoor Plants *(Timber Press, 1988).*

Epiphyllum oxypetalum, night blooming cereus, is a dramatic nocturnal bloomer. Bud formation is initiated by cool autumn temperatures. The aroma of dozens of perfumed flowers is something worth waiting for.

sights are different and sounds seem magnified. But, most important, my nose is greeted by a new collection of scents. After dark, when most flowers lack luster and their aromas fade, night-blooming blossoms begin their display. My greenhouse is filled with a heady elixir of floral perfumes.

I meet a lot of odd fellows after dark. Flowers of the night are typically large and luminous. And the aromas they emit are strange and strong. But, that's not surprising considering that they are trying to attract night-flying insects and bats. Apparently, creatures of the night prefer oversized blossoms and larger-than-life fragrances that a human nose might find a little overwhelming.

Perhaps the best known night bloomer is the dramatic night-blooming cereus. In fact, several members of the cactus family have earned that name due to their nocturnal habits. *Hylocereus undatus* is the most popular night-blooming cereus. In its native Brazil, that climbing succulent is courted by bats who eagerly attend its opening.

The blossoms of hylocereus open only once a year and tarry for only a single evening; they unfurl after dark and fade by daybreak. At 10:00 p.m. they begin to slowly unfold. Finally, an hour later, many foot-wide blossoms are dangling in the air. Each blossom is a frilly mass of creamy white inner petals and powdery yellow stamens. And every flower emits a sweet but cloying aroma to attract its specialized pollinators.

It takes many years for a hylocereus to reach blooming size. But, when it does bloom, the plant is definitely a conversation piece. Like other members of the cactus family, a hylocereus can tolerate a dry home environment as long as it receives bright light. Unfortunately, the plant with its thick, three-ridged stems is a little large for the average home. Most gardeners keep hylocereus in the greenhouse.

Epiphyllum oxypetalum puts on a similar show and shares the name of the night-blooming cereus. Although I wouldn't call it dainty, its broad, flat stems are a little more manageable in a home environment.

Epiphyllum oxypetalum specializes in drama. Triggered by cool temperatures, this succulent forms many tiny buds in the terminal notches of its leaves. The buds initiate throughout the summer, but cease growth at the same size. Then, when the temperatures begin to drop in autumn, the buds swell in unison to mature a month later and open simultaneously. The sight is well worth the waiting — the aroma of dozens of perfumed flowers is even more memorable.

An equally famous nocturnal bloomer is the popular lady-of-the-night orchid with its profusion of white, spiderlike blossoms and characteristically insipid scent. *Brassavola nodosa* remains open both day and night, although its three-inch wide blossoms are only scented after dark. Their smell is not exactly inviting, but the scent does have a certain tawdry "come hither" quality.

Brassavola nodosa is one of the easier-to-grow members of a notoriously difficult family. Not only is its compact habit conveniently apartment sized, but this orchid thrives in a home environment. The Lady-of-the-Night requires at least five hours of bright natural light or 14 hours of fluorescent light daily. Wire its small pseudobulbs to a bark slab, and water thoroughly twice a week, allowing the bark to dry out completely between waterings. With proper care, your brassavola should blossom in autumn. After blooming, rest the orchid for two weeks by withholding water.

Many gardeners don't realize that *Allamanda cathartica* 'Williamsii' is fragrant at night. The allamanda is a rambunctious vine that climbs rapidly and can be trained on a large trellis. Its four-to-five-inch wide, bright yellow, trumpet-shaped flowers appear in masses throughout the year providing quite a show. By day, the petals bend back, at night they lay flat and a delightful, delicate, Manischewitz winelike aroma wafts from the blossoms. The fragrance is an added attraction for a stunning plant.

Equally floriferous and famed far and wide for its nightly entertainment, angel's trumpets also put on a no-holds-barred, year-round performance. Angel's trumpets are in the *Brugmansia* genus (formerly known as *Datura*) and their oversized, dangling trumpets come in several pastel shades. Of all the relatives, the ghostly white *Brugmansia suaveolens* beats other colors in popularity polls.

A few stray blossoms adorn angel's trumpets throughout the month, but on alternate full moons, *Brugmansia suaveolens* really brings down the house. Hundreds of foot-long flowers dangle from the small tree. Each flower glows, illuminated by the light of the moon. By day the flowers are limp, but after dark they swell and emit a musky, honey scent that fills the air.

Every part of the brugmansia is poisonous. In small doses, the plant was once employed as an anesthetic during minor surgery. If consumed in larger quantities, a deadly stupor results. Primitive tribes often employed members of this family in their rituals. South American Indians administered it to youths during initiation ceremonies. The drug induced comas in the young men during which they were expected to forget their boyhood and receive their forefathers' teachings. In Columbia, a drink of datura was administered to the wives and slaves of a dead man before they were buried alive in their master's tomb. In South America, many people still believe that death will haunt anyone who sleeps under a brugmansia tree.

Brugmansias are sizeable plants, but they blossom easily and can be pruned to fit in a home. They need sun to blossom — a southern window would be ideal. Rather than continually repotting, fertilize generously and keep it potbound. Periodic root and foliar pruning will maintain discipline.

Another famed night performer is the night-blooming jasmine, *Cestrum nocturnum*. Unlike many of its fellow evening bloomers, cestrum has a delightfully sugar-sweet aroma.

The fragrance is heady, and a little potent in large doses.

Cestrum flowers are insignificant compared to most other night-blooming plants. In fact, the night-blooming jasmine is not related to the real jasmine at all; it shares only a similar scent. Its tiny, fragrant flowers look like long oboes.

Cestrum nocturnum is a large bush that can become unkempt if allowed to grow unchecked. It blossoms in summer, so you can safely keep it heavily pruned in winter and then allow the tips to shoot out in June. Full sun is necessary for producing a handsome plant and encouraging blossoms.

Nocturnal aromas are one of the small pleasures that reward gardeners who tarry with their plants after dark. At night, nature puts on some of her most dramatic performances. ❧

Sources

Check first with your local florist or garden center. Each of the specialty companies listed below carry some of the plants mentioned in the article.

The Fragrant Path
P.O. Box 328, Fort Calhoun, Nebr. 68023
(Catalog $1.00)

Glasshouse Works
Church St., P.O. Box 97, Stewart, Ohio 45778-0097
(Catalog $1.50)

Kartuz Greenhouses
1408 Sunset Dr., Vista, Calif. 92083
(Catalog $2.00)

Logee's Greenhouses
55 North St., Danielson, Conn. 06239
(Catalog $3.00)

Louisiana Nursery
Rte. 7, Box 43, Opelousas, La. 70570
(Catalog $3.50)

Stallings Nursery
910 Encinitas Blvd., Encinitas, Calif. 92024
(Free catalog)

Well-Sweep Herb Farm
317 Mt. Bethel Rd., Port Murray, N.J. 07865
(Catalog $1.00)

Preserving Garden Fragrance

Connie Krochmal

A bouquet of dried roses will last throughout the winter months preserving the beauty of the growing season.

Once considered necessary to protect health and combat unpleasant odors, garden sachets and potpourris made from the aromatic flowers and herbs grown in home gardens are now used for enjoyment rather than sanitation. Many gardeners prepare them as gifts for friends and family; they also preserve the aromatic fragrance of the garden over the winter.

The wonderfully fresh plant perfume that potpourri can provide is enough to help chase away the winter blahs, even on the worst days. Because our reactions to pleasant and familiar aromas are closely tied to our emotions, we can, through our senses, be transported back to the summer when the garden was at its peak of beauty. This in turn brings to mind the growing season ahead.

The home garden is an excellent source of flowers and herbs that can be made into fragrant products. Dried materials can be bought to supplement those from the garden. If space is available, you may want to establish a separate area for the aromatics; this will keep the garden proper from looking slightly bare as materials are harvested. A garden for such har-

Connie Krochmal, who lives in Asheville, North Carolina, is the author of A Guide to Natural Cosmetics, *(Quadrangle/The New York Times, 1973). She and her husband, Arnold, have published numerous books and articles on horticultural subjects, including* A Naturalist's Guide to Cooking with Wild Plants *(Quadrangle/The New York Times, 1975), and they write a regular garden column for* The San Juan Star, *Puerto Rico.*

vesting is sometimes known as a cutting garden. It may be well to put it out of view, because the continuous cutting will leave it looking a little informal.

A cutting garden requires the same kind of preplanting planning as a vegetable garden. Since it won't be a part of the planned landscape, it can be set out in an arrangement of rows and plantings that best suits the working habits of the gardener. Some people like to use long rows so that the soil between them can be easily tilled. The rows can be narrow, for single row planting, or wider, for double row planting, provided the plants can be kept within arms' reach for harvesting. Determine the amount of space between plants by the size of the mature plants; there must be enough space to allow for good air circulation, which helps control disease.

If at all possible avoid using pesticides and fungicides, since residues might be present at harvest. Prevention is the most important control. Provide the plants with good care, adequate water and fertilizer. A healthy plant is far more likely to survive problems than a plant which is not receiving sufficient moisture and nutrients. When you do water, water thoroughly, allowing the soil to dry out before watering again; too much water is as harmful as too little. Watering once a week should be adequate if you get the soil moist to a depth of five or six inches. It is a good idea to test the soil for fertilizer requirements. The State Agricultural Extension Services at Land Grant colleges will do this for a nominal charge, and there are also inexpensive soil testing kits which anyone can easily use. A fertilizer too high in nitrogen (the first number listed on the bag) is not recommended because it can interfere with and reduce flowering, since vegetative growth responds to nitrogen, N. Aromatic herbs, in particular, can suffer excessive growth, and consequently, reduced fragrance and flavor.

Sanitation is also important in protecting the plants' well being. Pick dead leaves and other parts off the plant and remove them from the garden area. Any plants that exhibit disease symptoms should be promptly eliminated.

Large insects can be picked off of the plants and destroyed. One very useful control is *Bacillus thuringiensis* sold under several trade names, including Dipel and Caterpillar Attack. Insecticidal soap spray is a good control for whiteflies and aphids. I use diatomaceous earth to control slugs and snails. All of these controls are toxic to specific pests, but won't harm beneficial insects.

If you plan to have a fairly large number of plants in your fragrance garden, it may be economical to start them from seed, if you have the space and time. However, if your garden is small, it may be more practical to buy what you need at a garden shop or nursery, as most packaged seeds are expensive. Some plants, herbs in particular, can be started from cuttings. Many perennial herbs can be separated, and this is another way of getting plants.

Planting time is determined by climate. Some annuals, such as stock, sweet pea, and mignonette, do best in the cool weather of early spring, and slow down or stop growing once the hot summer weather arrives. If you live in a cool climate, set tender plants out after the danger of frost is gone unless you plan on covering them when frosts threaten. Plastic minigreenhouses, called cloches, which are very lightweight, can be used for early planting protection. I use them, and in each one I put a couple of quart jars filled with water as solar collectors to keep the temperature up at night. Large glass jars can be used to cover individual plants, but they must be removed to avoid heat buildup during the day. Some people cut off the pouring ends of gallon plastic jars and use the rest as miniature, one-plant cloches to cover plants.

Picking the Flowers and Herbs

Harvesting must be done regularly once the plants reach the appropriate stage of maturity. Flower fragrance is strongest when the flower has just opened, and dissipates quickly in the heat of the day. Honeysuckles, which are more aromatic in the evening, are exceptions. Late evening and early morning are probably the best times to harvest flowers and herbs; at midday the warmth reduces the scent.

Most herbs, with the exception of lavender, thyme, and rosemary, should be harvested before blooming, when their fragrance is strongest. If flowers do appear, try not to let them remain on the plant beyond first bloom. If something, such as rain, makes harvesting impossible for several days, cut the flowers as soon as you can, as leaving them on the plant leads to seed production, and can also result in disease buildup.

Drying

Some of the aromatic products are better if made from fresh materials, while others are better when dried, then mixed. The fresh plant is generally used is making floral waters, colognes or herb vinegars, but for many herbal products, such as cosmetics, mouth-washes, and herbal bath bouquets, either fresh or dried plants may be used, depending on the particular formula. Rose water is made from petals preserved in salt.

If the materials are to be dried and mixed, special care is needed to prolong the fragrance. Drying in direct sun can reduce fragrance as well as bleach color. A temperature of 70° to 90°F. is about right. Air circulation is important; this can be provided by a small house fan, set on low to avoid gusts. I use a solar drying box with several trays, in a screened porch (see drawing). When the plants are ready they should feel dry and somewhat brittle. If they are to be used for a moist potpourri they are usually dried for only about 24 hours.

As the materials reach the desired stage remove and store in separate containers, in a dark, cool place. I prefer sealed glass jars to plastic bags, as the materials age somewhat in bags.

Preparing the Products

It is not always necessary to measure carefully, or have exact proportions, when making herbal products. Personal preference and availability of materials will determine the amounts. In an herbal or floral liquid mixture, the ingredients should balance, with a sufficient quantity of plants well dispersed in the liquid. Initially strong-scented materials should be used sparingly so they don't overwhelm milder scents. A general rule for most potpourris is between three-quarters and seven-eighths flowers, and the remainder leaves.

Avoid isopropyl or rubbing alcohol, as it can detract from the product by its own strong smell; instead use ethyl alcohol, which is available at pharmacies.

The methods given here, which should be easy to follow, allow room for trial and error and individual creativity. Keep in mind that if you are not pleased with a final product, it may still be usable. For example, a floral water with a very faint aroma, too weak to use as a body wash, can be diluted with a small amount of water, boiled for a few minutes, and then used as a liquid room freshener.

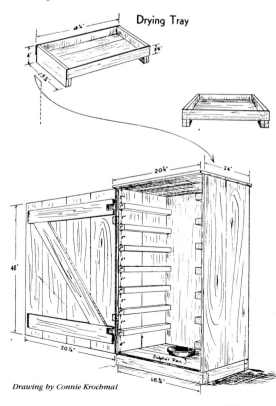

Drying Tray

Drawing by Connie Krochmal

Floral Waters

Place the flowers or herbs in a clean jar, add enough alcohol to cover. Seal and set in a dark place, such as a closet or cabinet. If possible, replace the materials every day for several days. When you feel the fragrance is strong enough, you may wish to stir in a little essential oil of the same kind. The final product can be used as is, or diluted with water, depending on the strength of the original product and your needs.

Floral Oils

Place the flowers or herbs in a clean jar, then cover with a scentless oil, such as corn oil (a strong smelling oil could compete with and distract from the plant fragrance). Follow the same procedures as above. You can remove the old plants by draining the oil through an ordinary kitchen strainer, and then returning the oil to the jar. The final product can be used as a bath oil, diluted with alcohol and used as perfume or cologne, or sprinkled lightly on a potpourri.

Herbal Vinegars

These are made in the same way as the preceding, but white wine vinegar is used as the solvent. When the aroma is as you want it, allow it to stand for several weeks before using. The product can be used as a hair rinse, or a small amount can be added to the laundry. For using on salads or in cooking, blending at a one to one ratio (or according to taste) with a white wine is suggested.

Herbal Cosmetics

A wide variety of cosmetics can be made from plants; many of them are covered in my book, *A Guide to Natural Cosmetics*. The following are a few of the numerous techniques that can be used.

To prepare an aromatic infusion of plants, immerse them in boiling water. Then allow them to stand for several hours until the infusion has the desired fragrance. Strain and discard the plants. This material can be used as the basis for several different products, including mouth wash, if you are familar with the

A nosegay composed of herbs will greet visitors when attached to the front door. These herbs will dry naturally.

plants (mint, for example) and know that they are safe. Sweet spices, such as cinnamon as well as sherry, can be used to give mouth washes a delightful taste.

The infusions can be used as skin toners and hair rinses. Witch hazel, in a proportion of about 1:4, works well as a toner for oily skin. To make an aromatic shampoo, simply mix an infusion with some liquid castile soap. The same infusion can be used for an herbal bath. Herbal baths, which are very refreshing and leave a light glow on the skin, can also be prepared by placing a small cheese cloth bag of plants under the faucet while running the water. About a half cup of dried fragrant plants will do the job.

A tussie-mussie — an attractive flower surrounded by aromatic herbs — is also a sort of herbal cosmetic. In Victorian times a lady going to a social event would wear one as a corsage; besides making her smell sweet, the tussie-mussie protected her from unpleasant odors.

Ornamental Fragrances for the Home

Dried plants have been used throughout history to provide pleasant odors in the home. Some dried herbs, particularly rosemary, lavender, sage, and southernwood, have also been burned as incense.

Dried materials also make handsome as well as aromatic indoor decorations. Lavender is a particular favorite. Cut the plants while in bloom, in bundles of about a dozen. Fold the ends over and tuck them in; this gives them the shape of "lavender bottles." Tie the stems together with a ribbon. Many dried plants can be tied in bunches like bouquets and then hung as decoration for doors or bedposts.

Sachets and Potpourris

These are probably the most popular providers of garden scent and fragrance in the house. Sachets are made of dried plants sewn or tied up in packages, usually pieces of cloth or handkerchiefs; these are placed in drawers, linen closets, or sometimes on the arms and legs of furniture.

There are two kinds of potpourri. Dry potpourris consist of dry plant materials kept in open containers. Moist potpourris, made of other kinds of plant material, are kept in heavy pottery containers and uncovered only when wanted.

Dry potpourri is made of dried flower petals, fragrant leaves, herbs, spices, seeds, essential oil or oils, and sometimes a fixative, such as camphor oil. Many kinds of ingredients can be used. I like a combination of about seven-eighths dried flower petals and one-eighth fragrant dried leaves. Too many leaves can overwhelm the floral fragrance. For each quart of dried mixed materials add about half a cup of fixative, camphor oil, or dried orris root and then about a tablespoon of some spice, to produce the desired aroma. A spicy or fruity aroma goes well in the kitchen. In other rooms personal preference decides what to use. Mix all of the ingredients gently to avoid crushing the flowers. A drop of essential oil, such as citrus oil, can be added. Place the mixture in a sealed container in the dark for three months to ripen. When it is taken out for use, place a few attractive whole dried flowers on top for decoration.

This sort of dried mix can be made into sachets or crushed and tied into cloth bags for use in linen closets. It can also be sewn into larger sachets, about four inches square, for insertion into pillows, which are called sleep pillows. The same mix, simmered gently in a small amount of water, will release a nice aroma into the home.

All varieties of spring hyacinth are fragrant. Not all daffodils are fragrant, but many are and will thrive undisturbed for years if planted in well-drained, root-free soil and fertilized annually as leaves emerge.

A moist potpourri is not intended to be decorative, as it has been mixed and stirred so much that it has a dark color and the component parts are not identifiable. The mixture is kept in a heavy ceramic or pottery container with a lid that can be removed to release the fragrance. Such potpourris are long lasting. Sometimes the ingredients are dried overnight before being placed in the pot, other times not. Dried rose petals are the main ingredient. Place them in the pot in layers alternating with layers of non-iodized salt. When the container is filled place a heavy plate or object on top of the petals. After a week or two herbs can be mixed in. You can also add a fixative—about one quarter cup to every four cups of plant material. Small amounts of essential oil, brandy, or cologne can also be mixed in. Stir every day to keep the ingredients in touch with each other, and be sure to keep covered. It will take several months for the fragrances to age and blend together. ❧

Plant and Seed Sources

1. W. Atlee Burpee & Co. Warminster, PA 18974.
2. The Cook's Garden. P.O. Box 65, Londonderry, VT 05148
3. Shepherd's Garden Seeds. 30 Irene St., Torrington, CT 06790
4. Sunrise Enterprises. Box 10058, Elmwood, CT 06110-0058
5. Johnny's Selected Seeds. Foss Hill Rd., Albion, ME 04910
6. Stokes Seeds, Inc. Box 548, Buffalo, NY 14240
7. Park Seed Co. Cokesbury Rd., Greenwood, SC 29647-0001
8. Thompson & Morgan. Box 1308, Jackson, NJ 08527
9. Shady Hills Gardens. 821 Walnut St., Batavia, IL 60510
10. Miniature Plant World. Box 7, Sardis, B.C. V2R 1A5
11. Pinetree Garden Seeds. New Gloucester, ME 04260
12. Nichols Garden Nursery. 1190 N. Pacific Hwy., Albany, OR 97321
13. J.L. Hudson. Box 1058, Redwood City, CA 94064
14. John Chambers. 15 Westleigh Road, Barton, Seagrave, Kettering, Northands, NN15 5AJ, United Kingdom
15. Heritage Rose Gardens. 16831 Mitchell Creek Dr., Ft. Bragg, CA 95437
16. High Country Rosarium. 1717 Downing St., Denver, CO 80218
17. Historical Roses. 1657 W. Jackson St., Painesville, OH 44077
18. Roses of Yesterday & Today. 802 Brown's Valley Rd., Watsonville, CA 95076

Sources

Flowering Plants

dianthus, annual or perennial *Dianthus plumarius D. caryophyllus, D. barbatus* 1, 3, 6, 7, 8, 11, 12, 13, 14

filipendula, perennial *Filipendula rubra* 12, 13, 14

geranium, perennial *Geranium macrorrhizum*

heliotrope, annual or perennial *Heliotropium arborescens* 1, 6, 7, 8, 11, 12, 13, 14

lily-of-the-valley, perennial *Convallaria majalis* 1, 7

mignonette, annual or perennial *Reseda grandiflora* 1, 3, 6, 7, 8, 12, 13, 14

peony, perennial *Paeonia* hybrids 1, 7, 8, 13

pyrethrum, perennial *Chrysanthemum coccineum* 1, 6, 7, 8, 11, 12, 14

stock, annual *Matthiola incana* 1, 3, 5, 6, 7, 8, 11, 12, 13, 14

sweet peas, annual or perennial *Lathyrus odoratus* 1, 3, 5, 6, 7, 8, 11, 12, 13, 14

valerian, annual or perennial *Valeriana officinalis* 12, 13, 14

violet, perennial *Viola odorata* 7, 8, 12, 13, 14

wallflower, perennial *Cheiranthus cheiri* 6, 7, 8, 12, 13, 14

wild ginger, perennial *Asarum canadense* 12

Particularly fragrant roses

R. centifolia cabbage or Provence rose 16, 17, 18

R. cinnamomea cinnamon rose

R. damascena damask rose 16, 17, 18

R. eglanteria sweetbriar rose (also known as *R. rubiginosa*) 13-18

R. gallica officinalis French rose 15, 17, 18

R. rugosa rose of Japan 8, 13, 15, 16, 17, 18

Annual Herbs

ambrosia *Chenopodium ambrosioides* 7

anise *Pimpinella anisum* 1, 6, 11, 12, 13, 14

basil *Ocimum basilicum* 1, 2, 3, 5, 6, 7, 8, 11, 12, 13, 14

camomile,sweet *Chamaemelum nobile*

yellow, golden *Matricaria chamomilla* 1, 5, 7, 8, 11, 12, 14

coriander *Coriandrum sativum* 1, 2, 3, 4, 5, 7, 8, 11, 12, 13, 14

hyssop *Hyssopus officinalis* 2, 5, 7, 11, 12, 13, 14

melilot *Melilotus alba* 14

perilla *Perilla frutescens* 1, 4, 5, 7, 11, 12, 14

sage *Salvia elegans, S. officinalis* 1, 2, 3, 5, 6, 7, 11, 12, 13, 14

savory, summer *Satureja hortensis* 1, 2, 3, 5, 6, 7, 8, 11, 12, 13, 14

scented geraniums *Pelargonium* spp. 7, 9

sweet marjoram *Origanum majorana* 1, 3, 5, 6, 7, 8, 11, 12, 14

Perennial Herbs

angelica *Angelica atropurpurea, A. archangelica* 8, 12, 13

bee balm *Monarda didyma* 7, 8, 12, 13, 14

caraway *Carum carvi* 1, 6, 7, 8, 12, 13, 14

catnip *Nepeta cataria* 1, 5, 6, 7, 8, 11, 12, 13, 14

clary sage—used as a fixative. *Salvia sclarea* 2, 12, 14

costmary *Chrysanthemum balsamita* 12

curry plant *Helichrysum angustifolium*

deer's tongue *Trilisa odoratissima* harvest from wild plants, southeastern US.

fennel *Foeniculum vulgare* 1, 2, 5, 6, 7, 8, 11, 12, 14

lavender *Lavandula angustifolia, L. spica* and other species 1, 2, 5, 6, 7, 8, 11, 12, 13, 14

lemon balm *Melissa officinalis* 1, 5, 6, 7, 8, 11, 12, 13, 14

lemongrass *Cymbopogon citratus* 13

lemon verbena *Aloysia triphylla, A. citriodora* 12

mints *Mentha* species 1, 4, 5, 8, 10, 11, 12, 13, 14

myrtle *Myrtus communis* 10

rosemary *Rosmarinus officinalis* 1, 2, 5, 6, 7, 8, 11, 12, 14

santolina *Santolina virens, S. chamaecyparissus* 6, 7, 8

savory, winter *Satureja montana* 1, 7, 8, 11, 12, 14

southernwood *Artemisia abrotanum* 12

sweet cicely *Myrrhis odorata* 8, 12, 13, 14

sweet woodruff *Galium odoratum* 1, 7, 12, 13, 14

tansy *Tanacetum vulgare* 1, 5, 7, 11, 13, 14

thyme *Thymus vulgaris, T. serpyllum, T. citriodorus* 1, 2, 3, 5, 6, 7, 8, 11, 12, 13, 14

Sources for Plants and Essential Oils for Potpourri
Indiana Botanic Garden
Box 5
Hammond, IN 46325

Caswell-Massey Co.
518 Lexington Av.
New York, NY 10017

Golden Meadow Herb Farm & Emporium
431 South St. Augustine
Dallas, TX 75217

Gilberties Herb Nursery
7 Sylvan Lane
Westport, CT 06880
203-227-4175

Books on Fragrance

Elisabeth Woodburn

From ancient times to the present, humankind has shown an interest in pleasant scents. Ancient paintings depict incense offerings, and medieval manuscripts record the fragrant characteristics of plants. The arrival of the printed book made it possible to record the plants from around the world that could please the sense of smell, as good food satisfies the sense of taste.

Before the age of plumbing it was common practice to strew fragrant plants to offset rank odors. Since lack of plumbing also indicated the absence of baths, it is easy to understand why householders were interested in the development of fragrant waters such as rose water and hungary water. Early distillers developed a method of preserving odors in alcohol.

Books on the development of perfumes record the many ways in which people have tried to preserve the fragrances they have found most pleasing. A popular work by G. W. Septimus Piesse, *THE ART OF PERFUMERY And the Methods of Obtaining the Odors of Plants*, which was originally published in French, then translated and published in England, and later republished in Philadelphia in 1856, is a good example of the transcultural interest in the subject. A number of scholarly studies on odors, fragrance, and perfumes were produced in France, Germany and England. The serious literature is extensive, but there are fewer popular works. The emphasis in almost all the literature is on the capture and preservation of fragrance.

Elisabeth Woodburn owns Booknoll Farm, a bookshop in Hopewell, New Jersey, that specializes in books on horticulture and agriculture. She is a founding member and former president of the Antiquarian Bookseller's Association of America.

Chinese witch hazel (Hamamelis mollis)

Books on the cultivation of fragrant plants are largely the efforts of twentieth century writers. This is not to say that writers in the past ignored fragrant plants, because the nineteenth century provided F. T. Mott's *FLORA ODORATA; A Characteristic Arrangement of Sweet-Scented Flowers and Shrubs, Cultivated in the Gardens of Great Britain*, in 1843, and, in 1895, Donald McDonald's *SWEET-SCENTED FLOWERS AND FRAGRANT LEAVES; Interesting Associations Gathered from Many Sources, with Notes on Their History and Utility.* The latter had an introduction by William Robinson and contained 16 color plates. It was sufficiently popular to warrant a reprint as *FRAGRANT FLOWERS AND LEAVES* in both New York and London in 1905. Its comprehensive listing of fragrant plants, their botanical names, habitat, and odor characteristics explained its popularity.

THE BOOK OF THE SCENTED GARDEN by a knowledgeable horticulturist, F. W. Burbidge, was published in London—and also in New York—in 1905. The fact that this was issued in a very popular and well-written series, "The Handbooks of Practical Gardening" indicates that the subject was appealing at the time. The 30 plus volumes in the series reflect the strong interest in horticulture at the beginning of the century.

The next volume in English appeared in 1925. This was F. A. Hampton's *THE SCENT OF FLOWERS AND LEAVES, Its Purpose and Relation to Man*. This is regarded for its description of the oils in plants, the functions of scent, botanical characteristics and color.

Eleanour Sinclair Rohde's *THE SCENTED GARDEN*, first issued in 1930 in London, was the forerunner of the modern books on fragrant plants. Miss Rohde, an able research scholar, discusses various types of aromatic plants, describes the best varieties, and includes recipes taken from the past as well as from the present. The book was repeatedly reprinted both here and in London. A revised edition in a smaller format was published in the U.S. as well as in London in 1948. It is still available in reprint.

A year after Miss Rohde's book first appeared, T. Geoffrey W. Henslow published *GARDENS OF FRAGRANCE*. A second edition came out in 1934. This practical work was devoted primarily to growing plants.

THE FRAGRANT PATH by Louise Beebe Wilder is most likely to remain the favorite among U.S. books on the subject. It was first published in New York in 1932 with a color frontispiece. It was reprinted (sans frontispiece) many times and is now available in a paperback reprint under the title *THE FRAGRANT GARDEN*. (Why titles are changed in reprints and imports is one of life's more annoying mysteries.) Louise Beebe Wilder, acclaimed as one of our most knowledgeable garden writers, wrote in an informal style that shares knowledge and friendship with the reader. Witness this passage: "Ancient books teach that the smell of many plants, rosemary among them, strengthens the memory, but none that I have come across calls attention to the trick that perfume sometimes plays us of suddenly calling up out of the past a scene, an episode, a state of mind, long buried beneath an accumulation of years and experience. How often the scent of some flower— honeysuckle, jasmine, lilac—stealing upon our senses in the night, causes the darkness to flower in visions of hallucinatory vividness." 'Smell,' wrote E. F. Benson, 'is the most memoristic of the senses'. Wilder's knowledge of garden literature is another enjoyable feature of her writings. She quotes the opinions of a wide variety of writers, giving them both appreciation and credit. Her knowledge of plants came from growing and observing them.

FRAGRANCE IN THE GARDEN by Anne Dorrance, published in New York in 1937, includes practical lists of fragrant plants for each season with tips for cultivating them. It is a small book which gives the impression that the writer noted the necessary information but did not "pad it". A quotation conveys this: "Unfortunately, as a word, smell has lost caste. Just the same the sense of smell, by whatever name you call it, plays a supreme rôle in life. Though we may call it fragrance, scent sweet and aromatic, though we seem to forget that opposites are there, we are still dealing with one of the basic factors of life."

The return to pleasure gardening after World War II brought forth a number of books which show that fragrant plants are increasingly appreciated for the added dimension they give to garden enjoyment. In 1955 in England Roy Genders's slim volume, *PERFUME IN THE GARDEN*, described various plants, giving descriptions, varieties, and information on their suitability for various uses. The popularity of this undoubtedly led to his 1977 *SCENTED FLORA OF THE WORLD*, which contained 560 double-column pages describing and growing facts about seeds, habitat, and cultivation of a large variety of plants. Genders also wrote *THE SCENTED WILD FLOWERS OF BRITAIN* in 1971, further proving his interest in the subject.

High on my list of favorite books is Margaret Brownlow's *HERBS AND THE FRAGRANT GARDEN*. She originally published it herself in 1957 as a 140 page work with 28 color plates that she not only drew but also ran off on a Gestetner machine she had on The Herb Farm in Kent. The public appreciation for this was such that in 1963 a commercial publisher brought out a greatly enlarged 2nd edition with 32 color plates by the author illustrating 318 herbs and shrubs. This second edition ran to 223 pages and had chapters on the quest for and the history, cultivation, and uses of herbs and aromatic plants. This edition also includes a reference section with a chronology of flowering times and classified lists of aromatic shrubs and North American herbs. There is an alphabetical listing of all the plants mentioned, with details of their characteristics, uses, propagation and culture. A third edition issued in 1978 was published in this country as well.

Norman Taylor, an American writer with many books to his credit, wrote *FRAGRANCE IN THE GARDEN* in 1953. This is a fairly brief introduction to the subject covering the essentials of planting and preserving fragrant plants in the six main odor groups used by perfumers.

Nelson Coon's *FRAGRANCE AND FRAGRANT PLANTS FOR HOUSE AND GARDEN* in 1967 included a thoughtful chapter on "The Invisible Garden"—gardens for the blind. Since Mr. Coon worked with blind people for a good many years he has made a number of observations that will surprise those who have not considered the reactions of the blind to

Fragrant lilies

A. Lilium regale, B. Lilium speciosum, C. Lilium auratum

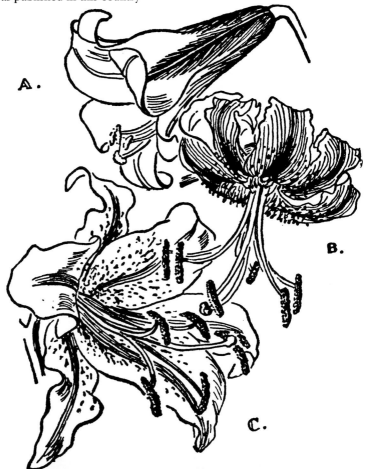

such gardens. Other chapters on the role of therapy, religion, and sex add more of Mr. Coon's viewpoints. The second section, "Fragrant Plants For Every Garden", lists many plants for various sweet-smelling plantings. In 1970 this book was brought out again by another publisher as GARDENING FOR FRA-GRANCE. This was not changed from the original.

THE FRAGRANT YEAR: Scented Plants for Your Garden and Your House, a book full of lovely drawings by Leonie Bell, includes her comments—especially on old roses which she found by searching early cemeteries. Helen van Pelt Wilson collaborated with her on this handsome work. The plants are discussed for their particular fragrances, best sites and seasons of bloom, and particularly good varieties are listed. The book was published in 1967 in New York and had a later reprint, also no longer available. Those who have had a chance to use the book search for copies of their own since it is both useful and attractive.

In recent years three appealing books have been added to the limited number of titles devoted to fragrant plants. All three were published in 1981. Frances Kelly's A Perfumed Garden, has special interest to us because it is an Australian publication. It enlarges one's fragrant plant palette by describing a number of Australian plants as well as more familiar ones. Her bibliography includes the English and American titles listed above. The charm of the book is greatly enhanced by Penny Dowie's pencil drawings and by four delicate color plates. Frances Kelly's writing is clear and direct. That it is popular is evident from the fact that a fifth impression of the book came out in 1984. The brief note on the author that appears on the dust jacket bears repeating "a journalist, poet, theatre critic, blurb writer, and member of the Commonwealth Film Censorship Board. She has written seven books on gardening and related subjects, also a play and children's stories. Despite all that she remains cheerful." This is the sort of humorous remark that makes Australia a great place to visit for the people as well as the plants.

Kay Sanecki's THE FRAGRANT GARDEN is adorned with four color photo plates, nine black and white photos, and 39 line drawings of plants by Rosemary Wise. The line drawings are particularly successful in their emphasis on the salient characteristics of the plants. The chapters are on fragrance and the plant, the love of scent, the search for scent, the centuries of growth, the fragrant garden emerges, and gardening with fragrant plants. The bulk of the book is devoted to a catalog of fragrant plants; this is divided into sections on greenhouse plants, bulbs, shrubs, green aromatics, trees and flowering plants. The book is interestingly written and filled with pertinent information.

Lastly, Rosemary Verey's most attractively produced book, The Scented Garden, is filled with color photography, color illustrations from old sources, photos and drawings comprising 34 color plates and black and white illustrations of over 170 of the 1100 plants listed. The plants are arranged by type—roses, flowers, bulbs, herbs, trees and shrubs, and exotics—with practical and historical information included. Both these last two titles were published in England; Mrs. Verey's work has been issued in the U.S. as well.

This list, devoted to books on fragrant plants does not even try to touch on the enormous amount of information on scented plants in a wide variety of other books. The old herbals are filled with notes on the scent of plants, wise men have pondered on the reason for scent, others have filled volumes with notations on the chemical elements that produce scent, and there are individual volumes on roses, lilies, violets and many other plants. The perfumers who use such vast quantities of the scented plants for perfumes and cosmetics have produced a large literature in many languages; these books cover everything from chemistry to manufacturing processes, with histories thrown in to supply the romantic touch. This summary should serve as a springboard for your own collection of books or notes on the books that you find most useful. To paraphrase an old quote on beauty—scent is in the nose of the breather!

Fragrant Bulbs

Deborah Peterson

Bulbs make glorious additions to any garden. There are bulbs for every season in a wide variety of colors, sizes and shapes. They are carefree, pest resistant, easy to grow, and you don't have to wait years for them to mature. With bulbs you can create a beautiful fragrant garden instantly.

The bulbs you purchase are totally self contained; the large succulent base will supply all the food necessary for one year. If you cut a daffodil bulb in half lengthwise, you will see that the tiny embryonic flower has already developed. Getting bulbs to repeat blooming is another matter altogether. Many hybrid tulips will not flower again and if they do, the flowers will be much smaller. Narcissus, crocus, muscari and many other small bulbs will repeat year after year.

Whether you are considering bulbs for summer or spring bloom, there are three categories, early, midseason and late. Typical of the early spring bulbs are crocuses and snowdrops, which bloom in late February or early March. Typical of the late-blooming bulbs are lilies-of-the-valley and iris, which bloom in May. Summer early blooming bulbs are the mid-century hybrid lilies, which bloom in June. Late blooming bulbs are *Lycoris*, which bloom in August. Most catalogs list bulbs by their blooming season.

Bulbs offer an enormous palaté of color, and if you study blooming sequences, you can make wonderful combinations. Early daffodils combined with blue muscari make a lovely display. Pink tulips and white daffodils blooming under pink flowering trees is another easy and attractive combination. The possibilities are endless when you combine bulbs with perennials that bloom at the same time.

Not all daffodils are fragrant so be certain to give them a nose test if seeking fragrance. Hyacinths are quite aromatic.

Spring Flowering Bulbs

Name	Color	Season	Hgt	Zone

Hyacinthus orientalis (Dutch hyacinths) All are fragrant.

Name	Color	Season	Hgt	Zone
	Pastels	Early	12"	4-8

Narcissus: (Daffodils) There are thousands of daffodils and many of them are fragrant. Listed here are those species known for their fragrance and some of their offspring. Unlike many other species of plants, narcissus do not lose their fragrance with hybridization. If the species is fragrant, there is a good chance their hybrids will also be fragrant.

Division I hybrids: These are the typical large cupped daffodils one thinks of naturalized on the hillside. Very few are fragrant.

Name	Color	Season	Hgt	Zone
N. 'Louise D'Coligny'	white/apr	mid	16"	4-8
N. 'Scarlet Gem'	yellow/red	mid	16"	4-8

N. poeticus: Pheasant's eye with a short cup, and white petals. The cup is frequently rimmed with red.

Name	Color	Season	Hgt	Zone
N. 'Actea'	white/yel	late	17"	5-8
N. 'Mega'	yellow/red	late	18"	5-7

N. triandrus: A charming group of slightly smaller narcissus, the petals are frequently recurved and each plant has at least three flowers per stem.

Name	Color	Season	Hgt	Zone
N. 'Hawera'	yellow	mid	8"	4-8
N. 'Thalia'	white	mid	16"	4-8
N. 'Cheerfulness'	white	late	15"	4-8
N. 'Yellow Cheerfulness'	yellow	late	15"	4-8

N. jonquilla: Another dainty group of miniature narcissus that are characterized by clusters of small, short-cupped yellow flowers. They are extremely fragrant.

N. 'Baby Moon'	yellow	late	7"	4-8
N. 'Sugarbush'	white/yel	mid	7"	4-8
N. 'Waterperry'	white/yel	early	12"	4-8

N. tazetta: This narcissus is characterized by a short cup and may have as many as eight flowers per stem. All are very fragrant.

N. 'Canaliculatus'	white/yellow	mid	6"	7-9
N. 'Geranium'	white/orange	mid	12"	4-8
N. 'Minnow'	yellow	late	8"	4-9
N. 'Grand Soleil d'Or'	yellow/orange	late	12"	7-10
(Can be forced without cooling)				

Tulips: Tulips offer the widest spectrum of color of any of the bulb genera. There are vibrant reds, deep purples, oranges, stripes and all shades of pastels. They do have one problem, rodents love them. In the hard winter months, nothing tastes better to a squirrel or rat than a tulip bulb. When planting tulips, put moth balls in the holes first and the tulips on top. The camphor does not hurt the soil or the plant, but it really deters the beasts.

Few tulips are fragrant. Those listed below are the ones with which we are familiar.

T. 'Bellona'	yellow	early	14"	3-8
T. 'Celsiana'	yellow	late	5"	4-8
T. 'United States'	orange	early	14"	4-8
T. 'Peach Blossom'	pink	early	10"	4-8
T. 'Princess Irene'	orange	early	12"	1-8
T. 'Apricot Beauty'	pink	mid	16"	4-8

Drawing by Barbara Bruno

Name	Color	Season	Hgt	Zone
T. 'Cheerleader'	red	mid	16"	4-8
T. 'Bestseller'	orange	mid	16"	4-8
T. 'Orange Bouquet'	orange	late	20"	4-8
T. 'Angelique'	pink	late	18"	4-8

Miscellaneous and small bulbs:

Name	Color	Season	Hgt	Zone
Ipheion uniflorum	blue	late	6"	5-10
Iris danfordiae	yellow	early	6"	3-9
Iris reticulata	blue	early	6"	3-9
Muscari armeniacum	blue	early	6"	3-9
Muscari botryoides	blue	early	5"	2-8
Ornithogalum arabicum	white	late	2'	7-10

Summer Flowering Bulbs

Name	Color	Season	Hgt	Zone
Acidanthera murieliae	white	late	24"	8-10

A lovely delicate bulb that is closely related to amaryllis. The flowers are white with red throats and borne on 24" spikes.

Name	Color	Season	Hgt	Zone
Alstroemeria	spotted	mid	3'	7-10

Large clusters of curiously spotted flowers in shades of orange, cinnamon, salmon and pink are borne throughout the summer. The bulbs must be dug in the fall in the North.

Name	Color	Season	Hgt	Zone
Crinum x *powellii*	pink or white	mid	3'	7-10

Lovely trumpet-shaped flowers are spicily fragrant and borne atop three-foot spikes. Crinums have an extensive period of bloom, from July through August.

Eucharis grandiflora: (Amazon lily)

Name	Color	Season	Hgt	Zone
	white	mid	2'	9-10

A wonderfully fragrant plant for pot culture in the North and a perennial for Southern gardens. Clusters of three-inch fragrant white flowers are borne throughout most of the summer.

Hedychium coronarium: (Butterfly lily)

Name	Color	Season	Hgt	Zone
	White	mid	3'	8-10

The three-inch fragrant white flowers are shaped like butterflies and are borne in clusters atop three-foot spikes. The bulbs must be dug in the fall in the North and stored over the winter.

Hemerocallis (daylilies)

There are hundreds and hundreds of hybrid daylilies but only a limited number are fragrant. Most catalogs will list fragrance as a quality. The practice, however, is to purchase blooming plants in the nursery. Here are a few with which we are familiar.

Name	Color	Season	Hgt	Zone
H. 'Hyperion'	yellow	everblm	48"	3-9
H. 'Classic Simplicity'	yellow	midseason	36"	3-9
H. 'Lexington'	cream	late	40"	3-9
H. 'Mary Todd'	yellow/or	mid	15"	3-9

Name	Color	Season	Hgt	Zone
Homeria	orange/yellow	early	18"	8-10

These are charming small bulbs for the front of the border. Their leaves are straplike and the flowers are pale pastels.

Hymenocallis narcissiflora   white   all season   2'   8-10
(Peruvian daffodil) Each two-foot stem has clusters of spidery white trumpet-shaped flowers with reflexed petals which give the plant a very unusual appearance.

Iris germanica hybrids: early   3'   4-9
The germanica hybrids are the tall bearded old fashioned irises of grandmother's garden—all delightfully fragrant. There are so many hybrids, and new ones are so frequently introduced, that there is little point to listing them. They come in almost every shade of the rainbow except red. They are a must for the June perennial border.

Lilium species & hybrids: (lilies)
Lilies are perhaps the most fragrant bulbs you can plant in the garden. However, there are so many species, cultivars and intergeneric crosses that it is almost impossible to neatly categorize them. The following are species and hybrids that are readily available.
L. candidum: Madonna lily   white   early   3-4'   4-8
L. longiflorum: Easter lily   white   late   2-3'   7-9
(This extremely fragrant lily has been doing well in NYC)
L. pumilum: Coral lily   red   mid   20"   4-8

Asiatic hybrids: early   20"   4-8
The flowers, upward facing, come in bright oranges reds and yellows and bloom in June. They are as fragrant as the above species. Examples are:
L. 'Enchantment' (orange), *L.* 'Connecticut King' (yellow).

Aurelian hybrids: mid   3-4'   4-8
The flowers are downward facing large trumpets and most, but not all, are quite fragrant. Examples are:
L. 'Pink Perfection' (pink), *L.* 'Golden Splendour' (yellow)

Speciosum lilies: late   4-5'   4-8
These are extremely fragrant lilies from Japan. The flowers are outward facing and fully opened. Examples are:
L. speciosum 'Rubrum' (deep pink), *L. speciosum* 'Album' (white)

Lycoris squamigera: pink   fall   2½'   4-8
The foliage appears in the spring and disappears in June. In the early fall umbels of lily-shaped fragrant pink flowers appear.

Pancratium maritimum: white   summer   18"   8-10
One of the most fragrant and exotic bulbs you can grow. The fragrant white flowers have arching recurving petals. In the north they may be grown in the garden in summer and brought in and stored over the winter. 🌿

For a list of public gardens devoted to fragrance send a SASE to: Publications Department, Brooklyn Botanic Garden, 1000 Washington Avenue, Brooklyn, NY 11225.